Lloyd's of London – a Portrait

LLOYD'S
OF LONDON

A PORTRAIT

HUGH COCKERELL

DOW JONES-IRWIN
HOMEWOOD, ILLINOIS 60430

Published in the USA by Dow Jones-Irwin, Inc.,
1818 Ridge Road, Homewood, Illinois 60430

First published 1984

© Hugh Cockerell 1984

ISBN 0-87094-570-X

Library of Congress Catalog Number 84-70597

Printed in Great Britain by St Edmundsbury Press, Bury St Edmunds, Suffolk

PREFACE

This book is an attempt to describe the institution of Lloyd's and its operation. It is not primarily a history, though it does contain a good many facts about the past because it is impossible to understand the workings of Lloyd's today without knowing how it has evolved over nearly 300 years.

Previous writers on Lloyd's have nearly always been members of the Lloyd's community. They have each had the advantage of an insider's knowledge and of the strong loyalty that membership of the community has always engendered. They have produced, as it were, self-portraits whereas I have taken a look at Lloyd's from outside as a disinterested spectator. One problem faced by all portrait painters is that the sitter will not keep still. Certainly Lloyd's has not kept still during the past year. It has hardly been possible to open a newspaper without reading of some new development at Lloyd's and much of the news has been distinctly unflattering. Much litigation and many enquiries are afoot, the results of which will not be known for months or even years. Besides this, the new Council of Lloyd's, constituted under the Lloyd's Act 1982, is only beginning to introduce new regulations and reforms. It could be said, indeed it has been said to me, that the time is not yet ripe for a new book about Lloyd's.

I respectfully differ. In my opinion it is a pity that no comprehensive description of Lloyd's institutions and practice has been available since C. E. Golding and D. King-Page's book *Lloyd's,* was allowed to go out of print some twenty years ago. It is true that there are excellent books available on aspects of Lloyd's. I need mention only the books of D. E. W. Gibb, Antony Brown, and Raymond Flower and Michael Wynne-Jones, which provide respectively an exposition of Lloyd's philosophy, a vivid impression of its operation, and an illustrated history. This book has a more practical purpose – to help the reader to identify the various organisations that make up the Lloyd's operation to see how they mesh together. The time is over-ripe for such a book, even though some of the Lloyd's machinery is due for, and is receiving, an overhaul. The state of affairs described is that prevailing early in 1983.

In painting on a wide canvas I may have got some details wrong. I shall be grateful for a note of any corrections for the benefit of a future edition.

Hugh Cockerell
Visiting Professor in Insurance Studies
City University Business School
Frobisher Crescent
Barbican
London EC2Y 8HB

CONTENTS

ACKNOWLEDGEMENTS

Mr Terry Atkins of Lloyd's Information Department has been most helpful in meeting my requests for information. Mr Adrian Lee, librarian of the Chartered Insurance Institute, and his colleagues have given me access to a mass of printed information. Miss Lauren Humphrey has typed the manuscript. I am most grateful to all three. It is I and not they who must accept responsibility for any statements in the book.

ILLUSTRATIONS

CHAPTER ONE

LLOYD'S OF LONDON TODAY

Lloyd's of London is tucked away in a side street. The stranger may not penetrate its portals without an introduction. Armed with one he can enter a large hall where 1 per cent of the world's insurances are transacted. This is a busy market place and one's first impression is confused. There are thousands of people. After a while it becomes clear that there are hundreds of desks, large and small, at the head or foot of which a varying number of people, from three or four upwards to twenty or so, are sitting on upright benches. The desks are arranged in long straight aisles along which people move. From time to time one of these people stops to speak to a man seated at a table and shows him a document. Some words ensue. Then often the seated man will scribble something on the document, apply a rubber stamp, make a note in a book on the desk, and give the document back. The other man walks off and goes to another desk, like a bee in search of honey, where the process with the document will be repeated. At some places there are people queuing up to speak to one of the seated men. The conversations, whatever they are, do not last long. On one side of the room, on a rostrum, is a man in a red robe who keeps up a chant of the names of people who are wanted on the telephone. Numbers light up on large screens like scoreboards at either side of the rostrum. Elsewhere there are notice boards with messages and sheaves of coloured slips attached to them. The doors are guarded by officials in red robes who are evidently there to keep out intruders. It is clear that something is going on, but what?

The Stock Exchange, which has a viewing gallery for the public, is easier to understand. There, the dealers, called jobbers, sit or stand at their pitches where a price list of the securities they deal in is displayed. They are approached by stockbrokers to buy or sell securities. Their price lists are always being marked up with changes, in blue if the price goes up, in red if it falls. The outsider can judge more or less what the trend of the market is. Transactions are said to take place on the 'floor' of the exchange.

At Lloyd's there are no price lists and it is impossible to detect a trend except to notice that the level of activity varies according to the time of day.

The trading hall at Lloyd's is called the 'Room', a modest description for a hall 340 feet long. The man in the red robe is the caller. The men at tables are said to occupy boxes, from the box pews of Lloyd's original coffee house. The principal man at each box is known as an underwriter. Those seated by him include a deputy underwriter and others who perform subordinate functions. The underwriter is he who decides whether to accept an insurance offered to him, and if so how much of it and on what terms. The offer is made to him by an insurance broker who comes to him bearing particulars of the proposed transaction, set out in a formal way, with numerous abbreviations, on a document called the 'slip'. If the underwriter decides to accept the offer he initials the slip and marks it with some letters and a number and an indication of how much of the insurance he is accepting. He is called an underwriter because at one time he signed his name at the foot of the insurance policy, the document which expresses the insurance contract which will ultimately be issued.

Underwriting members

Outside Lloyd's, insurance is transacted by insurance companies with capital provided by shareholders whose liability under the companies' contracts is limited for each shareholder to the amount of capital that he or she has subscribed. Lloyd's proceeds on a different and older basis. It is not a limited company at all. Instead it is a society, or club, of some 20,000 individuals called underwriting members, or 'Name(s)'. Each underwriting member accepts unlimited liability for his share of any insurance accepted on his behalf in the Room. This liability arises only in respect of his share. He is not liable for the shares in an insurance of any other underwriting member, but for his own share he must answer with the whole of his fortune if necessary. The holder of a Lloyd's policy may find that thousands of underwriting members have accepted a fraction of his total insurance. He is insured *at* Lloyd's by these underwriting members individually, but not *with* Lloyd's. It is true that there is a Society, or Corporation, of Lloyd's made up of all the underwriting members, but this corporation does not itself effect any insurance. It simply runs the market place and performs various services for the members. If a claim arises under a Lloyd's policy the policyholder must look for his money to the particular underwriters concerned in his policy.

Underwriting syndicates

The 20,000-odd underwriting members are like the shareholders of a company in that they provide the capital on the strength of which insurance is written at Lloyd's. They obviously cannot all themselves attend Lloyd's and decide which insurances to accept. This function is performed for them by a professional, called an active underwriter, to whom certain underwriting members have delegated power to act on their behalf. Those who do so form a syndicate which may consist of anything from two members to 3,000 or more. So when an active underwriter initials a slip he does so on behalf of the members of the syndicate of which he may or may not be himself a member, though he usually is. A syndicate differs from a partnership in that a partner is responsible for all the debts of the partnership whereas in a syndicate each member accepts liability for only his stated share of the syndicate's business. He receives his stated proportion of the premium due to the syndicate and is liable for the same proportion only of any claim. For an insurance of any size a number of syndicates are likely to share in the risk, so that hundreds or even thousands of underwriting members will be involved, each for a tiny fraction of the insurance in question.

There are over 400 underwriting syndicates at Lloyd's, classified according to the class of business they transact into marine, non-marine, aviation, motor and life. An underwriting member, in order to spread his risk, usually joins three or four syndicates. Each box at Lloyd's bears its syndicate number. Boxes are grouped according to the class of business transacted.

The active underwriter of each syndicate is the key man. It is he who decides on behalf of his syndicate how much of a given insurance to accept, at what rate of premium, and subject to what conditions. His actions govern the underwriting fortunes of the members of his syndicate, who by convention do not question his judgement or seek to influence his underwriting decisions. The remedy for any underwriting member who is dissatisfied is to leave the syndicate at the end of the year for which it is formed, as syndicates are reconstituted annually.

Lloyd's brokers

Underwriters are entirely dependent on insurance brokers for their flow of business. Only those insurance brokers who are approved by Lloyd's have entry to the Room. About 270 firms are so approved. They vary in size from the one or two-man concern to very large companies with thousands of employees in the United Kingdom and a network of offices or associated concerns overseas. These 270 firms are called Lloyd's brokers and can show with their address on their writing paper the magic words 'and at Lloyd's'. A non-Lloyd's broker might put such a phrase as 'Insurance arranged at Lloyd's', but he has to act through a Lloyd's broker. (There are special arrangements for motor insurance, as described in Chapter 8.)

Insurance brokers differ from other kinds of insurance agents in that a broker acts on behalf of his client who wishes to place an insurance whereas an insurance agent outside the Lloyd's system acts on behalf of the insurance company in getting business. By the custom of Lloyd's the broker accepts liability to the underwriter for the premium payable on any insurance placed at Lloyd's and the underwriter can if necessary sue him for payment, which he must make even if for any reason he finds that he cannot recover the premium from his client. Claims are notified through the broker to the underwriter and the underwriter will settle them in his account with the broker. The client has, however, the right to sue the underwriter direct for payment of a claim or for any return of premium that may become due to him under a policy, as when, say, an insured ship is laid up for part of the term of insurance.

When a Lloyd's broker receives an enquiry for an insurance he must find out from his client all the material facts that a prudent underwriter would require to know when considering whether to grant an insurance and if so on what terms. A proposer is under a legal duty to disclose all material facts to an underwriter because insurance contracts are a class of contract that requires both parties to exercise the utmost good faith towards each other. The reasoning is that the proposer knows all about the risk whereas the insurer knows nothing. It is only just that the insurer should be put in possession of the requisite information.

The broker puts the material facts on a slip for the underwriter to see and goes into the Room in search of suitable underwriters. He will first approach someone who he thinks will be willing to 'lead' the slip, that is, to take the first slice (called a 'line') of cover. According to the nature of the business offered he will decide whom to approach. Some active underwriters, by reason of their knowledge and experience of a particular type of insurance, will acquire a reputation as potential leading underwriters for that class. Others, who may well know less about it, will be content to follow their lead and accept a line of the insurance offered. If the broker considers the rate quoted by the first underwriter he approaches is too high, he will seek alternative quotations from others. Once he has settled a rate with a leading underwriter he will have to go from one underwriting box to another until the slip is fully subscribed. When this is done he closes the transaction and prepares a policy which is submitted to the Lloyd's Policy Signing Office. There the policy wording is checked against the slip. If found in order the policy will be signed. The policy quotes the official numbers of the syndicates concerned in it and refers to a list of syndicates which states the shares in each syndicate of each underwriting member. Lloyd's Policy Signing Office will also notify the underwriters of the transaction for both statistical and accounting purposes. There is a central accounting system which takes care of all the transactions between underwriters and brokers. This will be described in greater detail in Chapter 10.

The slip procedure has to be repeated whenever there is a modification to an insurance in the course of its term or on renewal. For some transactions the procedure can be too cumbersome and various devices are used. By way of example, it may be agreed in advance that modifications need only the approval of the leading underwriter. Again, brokers may be authorised to write business of a defined class, such as household insurances, on the underwriter's behalf and subject to his guidelines. Alternatively in, say, marine cargo insurance, an open policy may be issued under which all shipments of cargo are covered, provided they are declared monthly to the brokers.

The underwriter's aim is to get the highest premium he can for the risk he runs. The broker, on the other hand, owes it to his client to get insurance on the most favourable terms possible. Between the seller and the buyer of insurance there is thus a conflict of interest such as exists between buyers and sellers in any market. The theorist might expect that there would therefore be a complete separation between underwriting and broking, but this has not been the case for centuries. Many Lloyd's brokers are underwriting members and many underwriters are directors of broking concerns.

Underwriting agents

In addition Lloyd's brokers often operate as underwriting agents. Underwriting agents may exercise one of two functions or both simultaneously. The first function is to find persons willing to become underwriting members of Lloyd's and to manage such persons' affairs. Such management includes submitting proposals for election, finding underwriting syndicates for the member to join, watching the syndicates' progress and the member's investments, and keeping his accounts. An agency that performs only this function is known as a members' agency. Brokers are well fitted to undertake this work, as their clients include many potential underwriting members and conflicts of interest can hardly arise. The second function is that of managing the underwriting syndicates. The work includes finding members to join, providing office facilities, choosing the underwriting staff and appointing the active underwriter, who is thus heavily dependent on the broker concerned (if a broker controls the managing agency) for his career. There is in principle the danger that the broker could lean on the underwriter to accept business that he would rather reject in the interest of his syndicate, or to take business at a cut rate to help the broker stave off competition from other brokers. Many underwriters say that this danger is more apparent than real and that they do not in practice favour the brokers who manage their syndicate, but to set any doubts at rest the Lloyd's Act 1982 provides that within a certain period insurance brokers shall divest themselves of the control of managing agencies.

To sum up what has been described, we have some 20,000 underwriting members of Lloyd's, who group and regroup themselves into over 400 underwriting syndicates, each with an active underwriter in charge who accepts insurances on behalf of the members of his syndicate. Every underwriting member binds himself to accept liability for a fraction of every insurance written by the syndicate 'each for himself and not one for another'. For that fraction his liability is unlimited. The business is marketed and serviced by 270 Lloyd's brokers, varying in size from the very large to the very small. Lloyd's is a market place for insurance which arrives there from all quarters of the world. Clearly the market needs an organisation to run it.

The Society (or Corporation) of Lloyd's

The organisation in question is the Society of Lloyd's, which was first incorporated by Lloyd's Act 1871. Its affairs have been conducted by the Committee of Lloyd's, consisting of sixteen persons elected by the members of Lloyd's, with a Chairman and two Deputy Chairmen. By virtue of Lloyd's Act 1982 the Committee has since 1 January 1983 been topped by a Council whose constitution is described in Chapter 9. Its functions are many. It admits members, approves Lloyd's brokers and underwriting agents, and exercises supervision over their activities. The Society also provides the market place and facilities needed for the transaction of insurance. These facilities include, for example, the maintenance of property, the provision of catering, the running of the Room, supplying intelligence and centralised policy-signing, accounting and statistical services. An important task is that of ensuring that as far as possible underwriting members should always be financially able to meet their commitments. Members are required to demonstrate that they have adequate financial resources and to make deposits as security. The premium income of each member is regulated in the light of his means and the extent of his deposits. Members also contribute to a central reserve fund held by Lloyd's which is kept available to meet the claims of policyholders if any member should default. The accounts of underwriters are subjected to close scrutiny ('the Audit') by independent accountants approved by the Society to ensure that the underwriters continue solvent and do not exceed the premium income they are permitted. The accountants report to the Society.

The Society also collects and publishes details of Lloyd's premium income and obtains certificates of solvency. The Department of Trade and Industry relies on the Society to monitor the solvency of Lloyd's underwriters, who are excused from making the detailed returns to the Department that are required of insurance companies.

All countries have legislation controlling insurance companies. The Society of Lloyd's has a department which monitors such legislation and where necessary makes special arrangements, so that Lloyd's under-writers are able to transact insurance emanating from the country concerned. In Canada and the USA, for example, premiums collected have to be paid into special trust funds that are held for the payment of claims from policyholders in those countries. Again, business in France has to be separately recorded. The Society assumes responsibility for ensuring that these arrangements are honoured.

Another service rendered by the Society is the provision of central claims-settling facilities through the Lloyd's Underwriters' Claims and Recoveries Organisation (LUCRO). The work of the central services will be more fully described in Chapter 10. The Society of Lloyd's has nearly 2,000 people in its service.

The underwriters in the various markets have formed associations of their own for technical purposes which operate under the umbrella of the Committee.

Lloyd's brokers used to have their own market association, which has now become, as the Lloyd's Insurance Brokers' Committee, a part of the British Insurance Brokers' Association, but which remains answerable to the Council of Lloyd's in Lloyd's matters. There is also a Lloyd's Underwriting Agents' Association.

Lloyd's share of the market

Until a century ago Lloyd's was primarily a centre for marine insurance. It remains dominant in this field, but nowadays has more non-marine insurance premium income than marine. Examples of non-marine business are fire and liability insurance. If we compare the business placed at Lloyd's with that transacted by insurance companies we find that in marine insurance Lloyd's has more premium income than the companies. In life insurance Lloyd's has only a tiny share, as it confines itself to insurances that run for at most ten years. In other classes of insurance the insurance companies almost always have the lion's share. Many large insurances, for example, those on oil rigs, are shared between Lloyd's and the companies.

The Lloyd's system, in which hundreds of active underwriters are free to exercise their individual judgement, is particularly successful in coping with unusual or one-off risks. In the mass market large insurance companies have the advantage of a branch network to cover the country. Thus, in motor insurance in the UK, the companies have four-fifths of the business.

Lloyd's flexibility has enabled it to penetrate the North American market to such an extent that over half its business comes from the United States and Canada.

Lloyd's, past and present

Lloyd's, like many British institutions, is a curious mixture of ancient and modern. Nobody can hope to understand the present Lloyd's without some knowledge of how it has come to be what it is. Before going on to examine in greater detail its present mechanism we shall devote three chapters to describing how Lloyd's has evolved over the last three centuries. Meanwhile, four examples will illustrate how the past lives on in the present.

First, the attendants in blue coats at Lloyd's are known not as messengers or porters, but as waiters, a reminder of the coffee house which was all Lloyd's was for its first century of life.

Secondly, entries in the loss book kept in the Room, which records ship sinkings and other disasters, are entered with a quill pen in copperplate handwriting.

Third, the form of Lloyd's marine policy until 1982 had remained substantially unchanged since an example of it was appended to an Act of Parliament in 1779. Most of the wording was even earlier in date. Only now is the marine insurance world modifying its ancient and in some respects meaningless wording.

The fourth example concerns a feature of the Room, the Lutine Bell, which hangs above the caller's rostrum. It is a ship's bell from the *Lutine*, a French frigate surrendered to the British in 1793, which became a British warship and served under Nelson in the Mediterranean. In 1799 on a journey carrying bullion to Hamburg, it struck the sands at the mouth of the Zuider Zee and sank. Underwriters paid for the bullion. A little was salvaged in 1801 and in the course of a further attempt in 1859 the ship's bell, weighing 80 pounds, was recovered and came to Lloyd's. At one time a single stroke was given to signal the loss of a ship. On rare occasions nowadays it is struck once for bad news and twice for good as, for example, when Prince William was born in 1982.

CHAPTER TWO

THE EVOLUTION OF LLOYD'S TO 1850

Early forms of insurance

The oldest form of insurance is marine insurance. Indeed, for centuries it was the only form of insurance. Originating in Italy in the early thirteenth-century it spread slowly to other parts of Europe. From 1547 there are records of English marine policies written in Italian. They covered ships or their cargoes or both and were signed by a number of individuals, themselves ship-owners or merchants, who accepted a share of an insurance 'each for himself and not one for another'. Thus a policy on a ship for £1,000 might be subscribed by a dozen individuals, each taking £50 or £100 of the insurance. If a loss occurred, the policy-holder, known as the 'assured', would have to seek out the people who had subscribed the insurance and if necessary sue each man individually for his proportion of the loss. Lloyd's still uses the word 'assured'. The modern term, used in this book, is the 'insured'.

This system raised two kinds of problems. First, the would-be 'assured' had to find people willing to grant him insurance and, having a policy prepared, get each of them to sign. It therefore became convenient to establish a place where underwriters, that is, people willing to grant insurances, might be easily found. In 1566 Sir Thomas Gresham, a financier who had often been employed in state financial business in the Low Countries by Queen Elizabeth I, obtained the grant of the freehold of a piece of land in the City of London on which he built an exchange as a meeting place for merchants and others. It was opened in 1570 and after a visit by the Queen in 1571 it was known as the Royal Exchange. It has remained on the same site ever since, though it has had to be rebuilt twice after disastrous fires in 1666 and 1838.

Gresham modelled his exchange on the Bourse at Antwerp, which was a centre for insurance, transacted under ordinances of 1537, 1549 and 1563. A number of European cities had so-called chambers of insurance and in 1574 one Richard Candler, a connection of Sir Thomas Gresham, obtained a grant from the Queen to set up a similar office which would prepare policies and register all insurances in return for fees payable to him. He operated from premises at the Royal Exchange. The grant was maintained notwithstanding objections raised at the time by petitions from the notaries public and from the thirty sworn brokers who existed in the City at the time. They claimed that it would encroach on business which it was lawful for them to transact.

A second problem was that of settling disputes in insurance matters. The judges appear to have found difficulty in knowing what the usage of trade was in matters of insurance and the Lord Mayor, when appealed to for information, did not help. By an Act of 1601 Parliament established a Policies of Insurance Court whereby special commissioners were appointed to hear and determine disputes about policies. They were to meet weekly at Candler's Office of Insurance, without fee or reward.

The Office of Insurance survived for over a century. It was to the Royal Exchange that Pepys went in the 1660s whenever he sought insurance. The Exchange was burnt down in the Great Fire of 1666 and the Office moved temporarily to Gresham's old house in Bishopsgate. It is clear however that the Office did not enjoy its planned monopoly of insurance. A writer in 1676 said that insurances were either public or private. He called public those that were registered at the Office of Insurance, because anyone on payment of a fee might have a copy of the policy. It was only such policies that could be sued on in the Policies of Insurance Court which operated there, but the common law courts also recognised the validity of private insurances which were not so registered and which therefore had the advantage of being a private matter between the contracting parties. The liking for confidentiality is such that we can be sure of the popularity of private insurance. Indeed, soon after the end of the seventeenth-century the Office of Insurance was to disappear altogether.

In the 1680s two momentous insurance institutions were born, fire insurance and Lloyd's. They were unconnected. Fire insurance was transacted for the first time in 1681 by a partnership in which Nicolas Barbon, a property developer, played a leading part. Stimulated by the loss of property in the Great Fire fifteen years earlier, he and his partners offered to insure buildings in London against loss or damage by fire. They operated on a corporate basis, issuing policies in the name of the Fire Office or, as it soon came to be called, the Phenix Office, after the phoenix depicted on the lead mark which was affixed to the properties they insured. In 1683 a rival fire insurance company, known as the

Friendly Society, started to compete. For nearly two centuries fire insurance developed as a business for corporations to transact, with no place for individual underwriters, such as those who wrote other forms of insurance. The insurance provided by individual underwriters was overwhelmingly marine insurance on ships and their cargoes, though from time to time they issued policies on persons. These personal insurances were to provide a sum of money if the person insured was kidnapped in the course of foreign travel and held to ransom or if he were to die during a short period, usually a year. Life insurance of this latter type was issued mainly to people going on a voyage with its attendant perils. It therefore had a close connection with marine insurance.

Little is recorded about marine underwriting in the later seventeenth-century. With the decay of the Office of Insurance it is clear that persons known as office-keepers existed to provide for the needs of those seeking marine insurance and that underwriting was emerging as a specialised occupation and not simply as a sideline for merchants and ship-owners whose main business was their own trading ventures. Each insurance transaction meant that somebody had to provide the services of seeking out suitable individual underwriters, obtaining their agreement to accept a particular risk at a given premium, preparing the policy, obtaining the signatures of the underwriters and, should a loss occur, collecting the sum due from each underwriter concerned. It would have been a convenience to all parties if underwriters could have operated at focal points, but where?

Lloyd's Coffee House

An answer began to emerge in the form of the coffee house. Charles II's reign was the great age of the coffee houses. Since 1652 they had grown swiftly in number and there were by 1688 over 300 in London. Many developed a specialised clientèle. One such was Lloyd's Coffee House, started by Edward Lloyd, a man of about forty, in Tower Street, not far from the Tower Wharf and the Custom House. Here he might be expected to acquire a clientèle with a strong maritime flavour, especially as English shipping had doubled in the twenty-eight years between the Restoration and 1688 when Lloyd's Coffee House first came into the news. It had probably been opened a year or so earlier.

In 1691 Lloyd's Coffee House moved to Lombard Street, closer to the financial centre of the City. It was to remain there for eighty years. Lloyd, a man of enterprise, began in 1696 to publish *Lloyd's News*, a modest sheet of general and shipping news, but it lasted for a few months only. Lloyd's also became an auction room for sales of ships and other property. We hear of a ship auction there in 1700 and by 1710 the coffee house boasted an auction-pulpit. Lloyd died in 1713 and was succeeded as master of the coffee house by his son-in-law, William Newton. The premises had become a centre for marine underwriters, though it was only one among several.

Lloyd's Coffee House thrived under the founder's successors. The key to its success at the expense of rivals is to be found in the provision of intelligence about ships for the benefit of underwriters. In 1734 the then proprietor of Lloyd's began to publish *Lloyd's List*, a newspaper consisting mainly of shipping news obtained from local correspondents. By a special arrangement their letters were addressed to the Postmaster-General and therefore cost no postage. The Postmaster passed the information quickly to Lloyd's, which was almost next door, so information published in *Lloyd's List* was as up-to-date as possible.

Developments to 1850

Marine insurance was not in particularly good odour at this time. In 1693 unprecedented losses of close on £1 million on nearly 100 ships in a huge Smyrna convoy had driven many merchant-insurers into bankruptcy when they could not pay under policies they had issued. A few years later when a ship called the *Vansittart* was lost, it turned out that the broker in getting the insurance subscribed had invented the names of two insurers who appeared on the policy. These failures were remembered when moves were made in 1718 to form marine insurance companies with substantial capital to transact marine insurance. The proposals were opposed by the office-keepers (as brokers were then known) and by many merchants and ship-owners who feared that the proposed companies would constitute an expensive monopoly. They were nonetheless carried into law by the Bubble Act of 1720. The Act sanctioned the establishment of two corporations, the London Assurance and the Royal Exchange Assurance, and provided that no other corporations, societies or partnerships might insure ships or merchandise against marine risks. It expressly provided, however, that individual private underwriters were not to be prohibited from writing marine insurance.

It might have been expected that the two chartered corporations would attract most of the business available as they were so well capitalised. This did not happen as the corporations proceeded with the utmost caution. The marine premium income of the London Assurance in its first ten years averaged only £26,500 a year and sank to £20,000 in the next decade. Corresponding figures for the Royal Exchange Assurance are not available, but in the years 1761 – 1765 its marine premiums averaged only £36,600 a year, falling to half that in 1766 – 1770. By then its annual profit on marine insurance was no more than £6,000. Between 1700 and 1780 British exports and imports roughly doubled. So the insurance market as a whole was slowly growing. The scope for private underwriters remained large.

In the search for private profit eighteenth-century underwriters had few scruples. Even in time of war enemy ships were commonly insured. In 1748 an Act forbade insurances on vessels or goods belonging to French subjects, though the insurance of Spanish subjects was not prohibited. Even this measure was opposed in Parliament. Then too, many underwriters were prepared to enter into insurances that were no more than gambling transactions. They would agree, in return for a premium, to pay out money on the happening of some event, even though the policyholder suffered no financial loss as a result of the event: that is, he had no insurable interest. In 1745 an Act prohibited insurances on ships and goods where there was no insurable interest on the part of the policyholder, but the gambling insurances persisted. For example, one could insure to receive payment of a sum of money if Parliament should be dissolved or war declared, and the lives of persons accused of a crime could be insured. There were even insurances on the sex of the Chevalier d'Eon, a prominent transvestite.

In 1769 some underwriters who disapproved of gambling insurances broke away from Lloyd's. They persuaded a waiter there, Thomas Fielding, to open a New Lloyd's Coffee House, where he published a *New Lloyd's List* in rivalry to the original one which lingered on for five years. The new coffee house was in cramped premises in Pope's Head Alley. In 1771 nine merchants, underwriters and brokers who operated there, agreed to subscribe £100 each for new premises. They formed a Committee, which in 1773 negotiated a lease of rooms in the Royal Exchange of which Fielding and his head waiter, one Tayler, became the Masters as tenants-at-will of the subscribers. The scheme proved popular. A new regime began, with the users of Lloyd's, through their Committee, having for the first time control over the running of the premises. By 1774 the old Lloyd's had faded out.

The move to the Royal Exchange coincided with the passing of the Life Assurance Act 1774, which forbade insurances of the life of another where the insured had no financial interest in the life, and we find the Committee in its first pronouncement on underwriting condemning the 'shameful practice' of such insurances as leading to the possibility of murder. The Committee did not however seek to control underwriting in any way. Its main activity was in the admission of subscribers, for whom one of the two rooms occupied by Lloyd's at the Royal Exchange was reserved. There were 179 subscribers in 1779. *Lloyd's List* continued to be published for the profit of the Masters. A Loss and Arrival book was instituted for the information of subscribers in 1774. In 1779 a form of marine policy, based on ancient precedents, was printed. It survived virtually unchanged for 200 years.

This period saw the development of marine insurance law, shaped into coherence by Lord Mansfield, the Chief Justice, whose judgments are still classic statements. He took the precaution of sitting at the Guildhall in the City where he had access to the advice of experts who understood commercial practice.

At this time the law also began to restrict the extent to which slaves could be insured in transit. An Act of 1788 rendered insurances of slaves void against risks other than perils of the sea, piracy, insurrection, capture by the King's enemies, barratry and destruction by fire. A further Act of 1799 provided that no loss should be recoverable on account of the mortality of slaves by natural death, ill treatment or being thrown overboard. Subsequent Acts of 1806 and 1811 prohibited under heavy penalties the insurance of slaves or slave ships at all, though some underwriters contended that this did not apply to ships under a foreign flag.

The marine insurance market was severely tested in 1780 when the Spanish navy captured fifty-five out of sixty-three ships in the East and West India convoy. Losses totalled £1.5 million and there were many failures among underwriters. In wars between 1776 and 1783, 3,386 ships were captured, to the detriment of underwriters. They continued to insure enemy vessels and goods. Even the prohibition on French insurances of 1748 had lapsed and was not reinstated until 1793. War can spell prosperity for marine underwriters. If risks are high so are premiums. In addition the first effects of the industrial revolution were making themselves felt. Exports and imports trebled between 1780 and 1800. This was reflected in premium income. That of the Royal Exchange Assurance also trebled. The Napoleonic Wars led to a boom in marine insurance. Cases were reported of insurances on blockade runners at £40 or £50 per £100 in value. The Committee of Lloyd's, which had shown little activity in its early years, began to meet more than once a month. In 1796 it decided to hold two general meetings of subscribers every year. There was an influx of new subscribers. The total rose to 2,000 at the height of the war. In 1800 it was resolved that only merchants, bankers, underwriters and insurance brokers be admitted, each candidate having to be recommended by two or more subscribers. In 1802 a large new room had to be rented at the Royal Exchange.

Lloyd's was beginning at last to behave as a national institution rather than as just the clientèle of a coffee house. In 1798 the subscribers voted £1,000 as a voluntary subscription for national defence. Gifts of silver and swords were made to naval officers, including Nelson, in recognition of their achievements. The Patriotic Fund, to provide such gifts and to help those wounded at sea and their dependants, was started at Lloyd's in 1803 with a gift of £20,000 from underwriters. Lifeboats were provided for British coastal waters.

It was not to be expected that the prosperity of marine insurers would go unnoticed. Would-be entrepreneurs chafed at the prohibition by the Bubble Act of 1720 on the formation of new marine insurance companies. An application by the Globe Insurance Company for a charter in 1806 was successfully opposed by the Royal Exchange Assurance, but pressure persisted. In 1810 London merchants petitioned for an end to the corporate monopoly or at least for a charter for the Globe, and Parliament appointed a Select Committee to consider the proposal. Lloyd's took the lead in opposition and underwriters and brokers gave evidence, from which we can get some picture of Lloyd's at the time.

Lloyd's, it was said, had 1400 to 1500 subscribers, of whom two-thirds underwrote regularly or on occasion. There were seats in the under-writing room for 400 or 500. Underwriters were also to be found in London outside Lloyd's, at the Jamaica and Jerusalem Coffee Houses, at the Coal Exchange and in private counting houses. There were private underwriters, too, at Glasgow, Liverpool, Bristol, Newcastle and Hull, though only the first two cities mentioned were substantial centres. The two chartered corporations did no more than 4 per cent of all marine business. often their rates were 20 or 30 per cent higher than those at Lloyd's and they effectively limited the cover they offered to £10,000 on any one ship. The corporations were reluctant to insure cross-risks, that is, voyages between two ports outside the United Kingdom. Lloyd's underwriters had no such inhibition.

Despite Lloyd's opposition the Select Committee reported in favour of ending the monopoly. A Bill was introduced to that effect, but was defeated in a thin House by one vote. The status quo was for the time being preserved. Repeal of the corporate monopoly came only in 1824 after the formation, by a powerful group of City interests, including Rothschild, Gurney and Baring, of the Alliance Insurance Company. Immediately another company, the Indemnity Marine, was formed with a board including twenty-one subscribers to Lloyd's. Its premium income rose rapidly to £200,000, although it made no attempt to undercut Lloyd's rates.

In the first part of the nineteenth-century Lloyd's suffered a long period of decline, its subscribers falling in number from 2,150 in 1814 to 953 in 1843. The causes were threefold. Rates fell by three-quarters when the war risks were removed. Insured values also tended to fall in the deflation of the times. And in a stagnant market the competition of insurance companies was increasingly felt. A writer in 1844 claimed that the seven marine insurance companies then existing drew to themselves more than half the marine insurance business transacted in London.

Lloyd's tenancy of the Royal Exchange from 1774 was interrupted only by a fire which destroyed the building and many of Lloyd's records in 1838. After a sojourn at South Sea House at the corner of Bishopsgate and

Threadneedle Street Lloyd's returned in 1844 to the rebuilt Exchange with 11,000 square feet for its underwriters, now reduced in number to 258. Under a bye-law introduced in 1843 a discrimination had been made for the first time between those attending the rooms who were entitled to underwrite there and those who were not.

Hitherto all principals, underwriters and subscribers who had entry to the Room were styled subscribers. Now they became members, a title used for the first time. All had the right to underwrite. Future entrants became entitled to choose whether they should be members, in which case they paid an entrance fee of £25, or subscribers, in which case they did not. Both the members and subscribers paid the same rate of subscription, 4 guineas a year, but only members had a right to vote at a general meeting. Three years later, in 1846, in order to raise money, it was decided to distinguish among the members between those who underwrote and those who did not. The subscription for underwriting members was raised to 10 guineas. This had the effect of showing for the first time how many of those associated with Lloyd's were in fact underwriters. The number in 1849 proved to be only 189, a minority of the members.

During the first half of the nineteenth-century Lloyd's made only slow progress towards strengthening the central authority of the Committee. As Wright and Fayle, the historians of Lloyd's, put it in *A History of Lloyd's*:

> The history of Lloyd's is a history of continuous growth and change; but no step forward was ever made until its necessity had been proved by some crisis in the affairs of the House. Lloyd's as a body has seldom looked ahead. It has confined itself to recognising and dealing with the pressing needs of the moment.

Thus in 1811, in response to complaints before the Select Committee of the previous year that some underwriters had proved insolvent when a claim was made, the subscribers adhered to a Trust Deed (the first formal constitution after more than a century of informality). Bye-laws were introduced to regulate more strictly the admission of subscribers. In the past all applications sponsored by six subscribers had been accepted. Now there was to be a ballot by the Committee which could summon and question candidates. Subscriptions had hitherto gone to the Masters. Now the Committee was to receive and place them in a reserve fund. But the business of the Committee continued to be conducted by one of the Masters, who drew part of his remuneration from the profits of catering and part from the publication of *Lloyd's List*, which the three Masters shared among themselves. Not until 1844 were the Masters abolished. The whole operation of Lloyd's then became subject to the supervision of the Secretary, who now drew all his remuneration for performing the functions of that office, and a catering contractor was employed.

In 1850 Lloyd's was little more than a club with a small membership which offered facilities for the transaction of marine insurance on its rented premises, but accepted no responsibility for its members' business or behaviour. The Committee, as club committees will, spent much of its time on questions of catering or complaints about non-members intruding. It would collectively interview applicants for the post of messenger boy and ballot on an appointment. It had recently appointed a retired naval captain as Secretary with a staff of nine. Its income was only a few thousands a year.

Lloyd's intelligence gathering

In one respect, however, it was a national institution as a centre for shipping intelligence, which it gathered for the benefit of its members, but disseminated more widely. The Secretary's office received, digested and published a mass of information about shipping movements and marine casualties, much of which was published in the newspaper *Lloyd's List*. Since 1811 the Committee had appointed firms and persons in ports throughout the world to keep it regularly informed of local happenings. It had no difficulty in finding people who were prepared to perform this service free of charge in the hope of commercial advantage from their appointment. By 1829 there were over 350 and the number continued to grow.

Another area in which Lloyd's had long been active was the provision of information about ship construction. Underwriters and shippers of goods need to know about the quality of individual ships. In 1760 underwriters formed a Register Society, which collected and published information about the age, building and construction of ships. The publication, known as the *Green Book*, was confidential for the use of members of the Society. In 1798 ship-owners took offence at a revised contents list of the *Green Book*. In their opinion it laid undue stress on the age and place of building of the ships. Accordingly the ship-owners started a rival register of their own (the *Red Book*), which they sold at a cheaper price and with fewer precautions about security of information. Competition resulted in both publications being sold at a loss. In 1826 a committee composed of ship-owners, merchants and underwriters reported in favour of a new system of ship classification and seven years later the merger of the *Green Book* and the *Red Book* was agreed upon. In 1834 *Lloyd's Register of Shipping* appeared for the first time. It was, and still is, administered by a committee including ship-owners and Lloyd's and company marine underwriters, but it is not and never has been part of Lloyd's, though Lloyd's nominees form part of its committee, including the Chairman of Lloyd's, ex officio.

CHAPTER THREE

THE MAKING OF THE MODERN LLOYD'S 1850–1951

The year 1850 saw Lloyd's first departure from its practice of having an active underwriter as Chairman. Robinson, a ship-owner, also an MP, had been a successful Chairman for the past sixteen years, but the Committee decided to seek a chairman with influential connections outside Lloyd's, even though that would mean a man whose time was not available for the day-to-day work of the Society. Thomas Baring, of the banking family, was chosen. He had been a member for twenty years and was a Tory MP who could have had a cabinet post had he chosen. He held the chairmanship for eighteen years and was succeeded in 1869 by G. J. Goschen, a young Liberal MP who had already held cabinet rank and was subsequently to occupy a string of official posts, culminating in Chancellor of the Exchequer under Lord Salisbury. Goschen was Chairman from 1869 to 1886 and again from 1893 to 1901 when he reached the age of seventy. In the years between, Lord Revelstoke, of the Baring family, occupied the chair.

The succession of 'political' Chairmen who could not always be at hand to deal with day-to-day matters stressed the importance of having a Secretary capable of more than coping with routine administration. The need for a Secretary of some weight had been recognised by the appointment in 1848 of Captain G. A. Halsted RN. During his twenty years of efficient service the secretariat was strengthened. In 1874 a young army captain, Henry Hozier, became Secretary. He remained in office till 1906. Hozier was a masterful character. He had the gift of picking subordinates and was, too, a man of ideas. For many years, while the chairmanship remained ornamental, he dominated the Committee. After him the office of Secretary retreated for many years into comparative anonymity, but he left behind an efficient administration which served Lloyd's well through the stresses of two World Wars and beyond.

Hozier's outstanding contribution to Lloyd's, apart from ensuring that the central organisation functioned smoothly, lay in his energetic development of Lloyd's intelligence services, at first by the greater use of telegraphy and later by wireless, which earned him a knighthood. These developments are described in Chapter 14.

Between 1850 and 1951 Lloyd's completed its evolution from a meeting place where people came to transact insurance at their own risk with the underwriters assembled there, to a market providing many central services and concerned with the solvency and conduct of its membership.

At the outset of this period the Committee confined itself, by way of services, to management of the premises and the provision of shipping intelligence. In 1848 Lloyd's had a central staff of nine. Twenty-six years later the staff had grown to forty-four and by 1951 it was approaching 2,000. The growth arose, not from Parkinson's Law, but from necessity. In one area after another central services had to be provided because they were found indispensable for the efficient working of the market.

Developments in the protection of policyholders' interests

In 1850 the tradition of relatively easy entry to membership still prevailed. Policyholders had to rely on brokers to select among Lloyd's underwriters those who would be pretty sure to meet their liabilities. If some should prove unable to pay it was just too bad. Nor did it follow that the insolvent or the potentially insolvent would be excluded. No one is recorded as having been expelled until 1828 and even in that year one member of the Committee dissented when it was decided to erase from the list of subscribers two brokers who had fraudulently obtained a return of premium from underwriters and failed to pass it on to their clients. Bye-laws passed in 1843 had given the Committee power to refuse to renew the subscription of a subscriber, but they had no such power in relation to a member who was responsible for underwriting. Not until 1851 did a general meeting resolve that if any member became bankrupt his membership should cease.

Lloyd's Act 1871

About twenty years later, in 1870, an unsuccessful attempt by the Committee to expel a member from whom underwriters were seeking to recover £500 paid under a policy he held, led to a High Court judgment that the Committee had exceeded its powers. The Committee decided to seek an Act of Parliament to make its powers clear. The result was Lloyd's Act 1871 whereby Lloyd's became for the first time an incorporated society.

The Act recited in its preamble that the business conducted by the members of Lloyd's was of large and increasing magnitude and importance, but that the constitution of the Society was imperfect and difficulties had arisen in relation to legal proceedings, so that incorporation with proper powers would be of great benefit to shipping and mercantile interests. Section 10 defined the objects of the Society as:

the carrying on of the business of marine insurance by members;
the collection, publication and diffusion of intelligence and information;
the doing of all things incidental or conducive to the fulfilment of the objects.

The Act provided for a committee of twelve, with a vote for every member. It set forth 'five fundamental rules of the Society', which can be summarised as follows:

1   There shall be underwriting members and non-underwriting members.

2   A non-underwriting member shall not underwrite in his own name at Lloyd's or empower another person to underwrite for him at Lloyd's.

3   All underwriting business transacted at Lloyd's shall be conducted in the underwriting rooms and not elsewhere.

4   An underwriting member shall not directly or indirectly underwrite in the City of London a policy
    (a)   otherwise than in the name of one individual for each separate sum subscribed;
    (b)   for the account of any company or association unless they are subscribers to the Society, nor unless every policy is underwritten in their ordinary place of business.

5   A member shall not open an insurance account in the name of any person not being a member or subscriber.

The Society was empowered to make by-laws which had to be submitted to the Recorder of the City of London and allowed by him.

A member convicted of fraud or infamous crime, or becoming bankrupt or insolvent, or suspending payment or seeking a composition with creditors, would cease to be a member. In all other cases of attempted exclusion on the ground of violation of a fundamental rule or discreditable conduct as an underwriter or in connection with marine insurance, the Act made it a pre-condition that there should be a finding of violation or guilt by two arbitrators and that the exclusion should be decided on at a special meeting, with a voting quorum of 100 and a four-fifths majority. A hundred and ten years were to elapse before the machinery was operated.

Life Assurance Companies Act 1870

The *laissez-faire* atmosphere of the mid-Victorian age had little place for state consumer protection. In 1869 however a large life insurance company had collapsed and Parliament passed the Life Assurance

Companies Act 1870. This required new life insurance companies to make a deposit as evidence that they had some capital. All life companies were required to furnish accounts and actuarial returns for publication. The system was one of 'freedom with publicity'. The state considered that it had done its duty by consumers if the facts about each company were made available, the consumer being left free to make his informed choice among them. If he made a bad choice he had only himself to blame. In non-life insurance the field remained open to all insurers for the next forty years.

Underwriters' security

At Lloyd's the first tentative steps towards securing policy-holders were being made at this time. It was clearly damaging to the market if any underwriter failed to honour his commitments, but the tradition of each man for himself was very strong. The Committee took no action on a suggestion by a member in 1855 that new underwriters should be required to give security. In 1856, it took a guarantee of £5,000 from a relation for H. J. P. Dumas on his election. In the following year it accepted a deposit of £5,000 from an applicant whose father objected to giving a guarantee. Between 1849 and 1870 the membership doubled. For the next twenty-five years applicants continued to be admitted at the Committee's discretion with either a guarantee or a deposit, or neither. A motion at a general meeting in 1870 calling for a deposit of £3,000 in all cases was defeated. It was only in 1882 that the Committee came to require a deposit or guarantee from all new entrants. The rate for deposits was settled at £5,000 and Lloyd's publicised their existence.

Meanwhile a new factor was emerging – Lloyd's growing participation in non-marine insurance, at first principally fire insurance. It appears that Lloyd's was prevented from transacting fire insurance in the United Kingdom until 1865 because the Inland Revenue recognised only insurance companies as agents for collection of fire insurance duty. The abolition of the duty in 1865 opened the door to Lloyd's and home fire business began to be transacted by underwriters, all of whom were primarily marine insurance men. Lloyd's Act 1871 referred to the principal object of the Society as 'the carrying on of marine insurance by members'. The Act made no reference to any other class of business.

Fire insurance, negligible in 1871, grew apace in the 1880s, thanks especially to Cuthbert Heath, a marine underwriter who started his own syndicate in 1881, with himself and another as members. One of his earliest decisions was to reinsure the fire business of the Hand in Hand, the oldest surviving fire insurance society. Heath was an innovator, always open to suggestions for novel applications of the insurance principle. In consequence other types of non-marine insurance developed at Lloyd's. Their growth was viewed with apprehension by more traditional underwriters. The Committee of Lloyd's took the view, on legal advice, that deposits and guarantees obtained from underwriters could not be applied to claims under non-marine insurances. It publicised this fact and decided that non-marine policies should not bear the anchor which had since 1871 been the trademark of a Lloyd's policy. For many years, therefore, non-marine insured received documents that were not in the full sense Lloyd's policies. It was only in 1902 that the Committee began to take deposits or guarantees in respect of non-marine business. Lloyd's Act 1911 amended the 1871 Act by saying that the first object of the Society was 'the carrying on by Members of the Society of the business of insurance of every description including guarantee business'.

In 1902 one Burnand, who underwrote for a syndicate of five members, became insolvent through guaranteeing, by policies he issued on behalf of his syndicate, the bills of exchange of a travel agency of which he was a director. Each member of Burnand's syndicate found himself saddled with a liability of £20,000. Burnand's case highlighted the fact that an active underwriter could spend the premiums he received as he chose, keeping afloat by using this year's premiums to pay last year's claims. In 1903 the Committee decided to ask every new underwriter to agree to put his premiums in trust for the payment of his underwriting liabilities. In the long run, and it could have been a very long run, all premiums would be in trust.

In 1908, largely at the instance of Heath, Lloyd's took further steps towards tightening security. A general meeting agreed that all underwriters' accounts should be audited by an approved auditor with a view to certifying their solvency and, further, that all premiums should be paid into a trust fund. The timing was fortunate as in 1909 a bill passed through Parliament to regulate fire and accident insurance on similar lines to the Life Assurance Companies Act 1870 which related to life insurance. The bill (later the Assurance Companies Act 1909) called for deposits of £20,000 per class of insurance from new insurance companies and £2,000 from every individual underwriter. The Committee of Lloyd's was able, thanks to its recently instituted system of audit, to obtain an exemption from the deposit requirement for any underwriter who could produce a certificate of solvency and had provided the Committee with a deposit or guarantee equal to a year's premium income. Lloyd's was given the role of making global returns in respect of the business of all its underwriters. In other words Lloyd's obtained a system of self-regulation for itself which has been maintained to this day.

The American market

The years 1850 – 1960 were a period of slow growth for a long time from a low base. In 1853 Lloyd's had only 257 members entitled to underwrite; in 1870, 401. By 1913 there were 621, writing marine insurance premiums of £8.9 million and non-marine of £2.5 million. Fourteen years later the membership had doubled, to 1,248. By 1949 it doubled again, to 2,590. It was the rise of American business from the 1880s, and of motor and liability insurances from the early 1900s that accounted for the subsequent phenomenal development.

Lloyd's reputation stood high in the United States. In 1892 New York State passed a law against the deceptive use of Lloyd's name by imitators. In 1910 there were still in that state thirty-seven institutions using the name 'Lloyd's' in their title. Impetus was given to Lloyd's reputation by underwriters' prompt and unconditional settlement of claims arising out of the San Francisco earthquake and fires of 1906, a time when many American insurance companies failed. The success of Lloyd's in the American market led to demands by American insurance companies for protection against competition by a concern that was free of the strict regulation they themselves underwent at the hands of state superintendents of insurance. American states began to prohibit the placing of insurance with a 'non-admitted insurer', as Lloyd's was, unless the business had first been offered to and rejected by admitted insurers in the local market. In Illinois in 1933 some Lloyd's brokers and underwriters found it necessary, if they were to continue doing business there, to deposit US $250,000, which they did. In 1937 the Committee of Lloyd's formed a company, Additional Securities Limited, to make such deposits in the United States or elsewhere when these were found necessary to enable Lloyd's underwriters to operate.

Non-marine insurance was for its early years, until 1900, transacted by marine underwriters, for most of whom it was an incidental. Because of Heath's high reputation as a leader and innovator in the market, marine syndicates were happy to follow his lead and accept a line on non-marine insurances. Heath's own syndicate also transacted marine insurance. It was not until 1902 that the first purely non-marine syndicate was established. Differentiation between marine and non-marine insurance remained incomplete. Non-marine underwriters continued to reinsure with marine syndicates, to their great advantage in the 1950s when serious hurricane losses arose in the United States.

The growth of reinsurance

The period also saw the growth of reinsurance, whereby one insurer passes over (or cedes) a part of the risk he has assumed under an insurance to another insurer (the reinsurer), in return for part of the premium. Reinsurance, except in certain circumstances, had been nominally illegal until 1864.

At first, reinsurance related to the whole or a proportion of the original insurance and had to be documented by particulars of each policy issued and each claim, with a resultant mass of paper. Lloyd's developed so-called non-proportional reinsurance, whereby the reinsurer, without concerning himself with the detail of every policy, undertook simply to pay claims in excess of an agreed figure in return for an arbitrarily calculated percentage of all premiums received by the original insurers. This simpler though riskier form of contract reduced clerical work to a minimum and saved the underwriter from having to support a large staff.

Lloyd's in World War I

World War I affected Lloyd's both in the nature of business transacted and in the way it was done. The War opened up a widespread demand for insurance of property at sea and on land against war risks. A government committee (the Huth Jackson Committee) had examined the problem in 1913 and made recommendations on marine war risks which were implemented on the outbreak of war. The government accepted 80 per cent of the risk on hulls, leaving 20 per cent to private insurers. For cargoes the government opened a state insurance office which offered to insure cargoes in British ships at a fixed rate. The government thus became, as it recognised at the time, an insurer of last resort; under-writers were left free to offer lower rates for any business they wanted. The result was foreseeable. Underwriters made large profits on the more desirable part of the cargo business and the state lost £7.5 million on the residue.

Insurance of war risk on land property was left to private enterprise for three years. Lloyd's took the lead in covering it as few companies were willing to accept the risk and of these one at least reinsured it fully at Lloyd's. Only in 1917 did the government decide to provide insurance, using insurance companies as its agents. The premiums under the scheme exceeded claims by £10 million. War risk business also proved profitable to underwriters.

Lloyd's had an influx of members during the War and the Room stayed open until long after 6 p.m. As practically all the young men had joined the forces a heavy burden was thrown on those who remained. One area where this was specially felt was in the signing of policies. It had always been the practice for youths known as policy pushers, or policy shovers, to take policies around the Room for signature by all the active under-writers whose syndicates took part of an insurance. Policies were left in a wire basket in the box for signature by the underwriter of the leading syndicate, then collected and passed on to the next syndicate. The process could take a long time with the policy emerging weeks later dog-eared or torn. In 1916 the Committee sanctioned a scheme whereby, as a voluntary alternative method, policies could be checked and signed on behalf of all underwriters in a Policy Signing Bureau which came to be staffed by girls. The system was obviously quicker and more efficient. Despite a temporary schism between marine and non-marine underwriters, who started to maintain two separate organisations, it survived the war. In 1924 the Committee assumed responsibility for the bureau, now the Lloyd's Policy Signing Office, and its use became compulsory.

Between the Wars

After World War I began the expansion of three forms of insurance that had hitherto been of minor importance only – motor, aviation and credit. Motor insurance will be referred to in Chapter 8. Aviation insurance made a slow start. Group underwriting by syndicates which included both Lloyd's underwriters and insurance companies was attempted, in one case with both subscribing to a single policy, but at least one such syndicate was dissolved in 1923. Credit insurance, that is, insurance of a trader against the failure of a debtor to pay him, also experienced growing pains despite the government's wish to encourage it. Its progress at Lloyd's was soon to receive a check. No system of regulation or self-regulation is proof against the dishonesty of individuals. In 1923 Harrison, a broker and underwriter with a syndicate of five Names, of which he was not one, got into hot water when on behalf of his syndicate he guaranteed bills for a hire purchase company, some of them relating to imaginary vehicles. He kept a separate series of books for these credit insurance transactions which were not shown to his auditors. When the inevitable crash came the Chairman of Lloyd's called a meeting of underwriting agents and asked all syndicates for subscriptions of £200,000 to meet all justified claims. The market provided the money.

As a direct result of the Harrison episode the Committee of Lloyd's decided to outlaw financial guarantee business. Cuthbert Heath, the pioneer of credit insurance, led the opposition to this step and the Committee gave way to the extent that while requiring underwriters to undertake not to write direct financial guarantee business it allowed them to offer reinsurance to approved insurance companies subject to various safeguards, including additional deposits. Heath continued to develop this form of insurance through outside companies he had founded.

In 1927 the Lloyd's Central Reserve Fund was set up, out of a continuing small levy on all premiums received at Lloyd's. The Central Reserve Fund is held in trust by the Committee of Lloyd's to pay any policyholder's claims that cannot be met out of the underwriting reserves and the personal fortune of any underwriting member. Thus it is a fund of last resort for the benefit of policyholders. It is not held for the purpose of relieving underwriters of their personal, unlimited liability and, in the terms of the trust, cannot be used for that purpose.

Lloyd's in World War II

Problems of insurance against war risk encountered in World War I were intensified when World War II broke out in 1939. On the non-marine side the insurers of the world had decided in 1938 that with the increased possibility of damage to property on land by aircraft they could not afford to take the risk. They all, Lloyd's underwriters and insurance companies alike, agreed that they would not offer the cover except in the United States and Canada. Marine insurers, by the so-called Waterborne Agreement, undertook to confine cover on cargoes on land to forty-eight hours after arrival. Inability to obtain cover for stocks of goods meant that the owners would be tempted to run them down to minimise their risks just at a time when it was desirable in the national interest that stocks (for example, of food and raw materials) should be maintained at a high level. The government therefore introduced a scheme of compulsory insurance for stocks which was administered on its behalf by insurance companies, the Corporation of Lloyd's and insurance brokers. The War Damage Act 1941 made similar (optional) provision for furniture, machinery and business equipment. The Act also imposed an extra charge on Schedule A of income tax on buildings – the government, without undertaking full liability for war damage, agreeing that it would try to meet claims. In the event all claims were met.

On the marine side it had become common since World War I for cargo-owners to insure against war risk subject to the underwriters' right to cancel at forty-eight hours notice in respect of cargo not yet shipped. In the early stages of the War an Act provided for government reinsurance of war risk on ships and cargoes. It was left to underwriters to insure these risks as they thought fit and to reinsure them fully with the government. In 1940, as the War intensified, the government opened its own War Risk Insurance Office. Insurers were in principle free to compete for cargo insurance, but by a self-denying ordinance they agreed always to quote above the official government rate; so far as concerned cargo to and from the United Kingdom, while retaining a free hand in quoting for cross-risks, that is, transits between ports outside the United Kingdom.

Two serious problems arose in connection with Lloyd's American business. The first came in 1939 when Americans feared that the British government in its urgent need to pay for American arms might requisition Lloyd's funds and so leave American policyholders in danger of not being able to collect their claims in dollars. Just before war broke out Lloyd's calmed these fears by establishing the Lloyd's American Trust Fund into which all United States dollar premiums were to be paid and held for the benefit of policyholders in the first place. A similar fund was later established for Canadian dollar premiums. The arrangement has worked smoothly ever since.

The second problem concerned security of information after the United States' entry into the War. Americans were concerned that information about shipping movements and land installations provided to underwriters in the course of their business might fall into enemy hands where it could have great value as intelligence. In 1942 the United States banned the export of information about ships' movements or any project or plant engaged in the war effort. The Chairman of Lloyd's visited the United States to seek a solution. This was found when Lloyd's set up a bureau in New York to which all the information necessary for underwriting marine or non-marine risks would be supplied. The bureau then transmitted to London only such information as was officially permitted and Lloyd's underwriters had to operate partly in the dark. Thanks to the expertise of the bureau's staff, experienced people sent over from London, the scheme operated successfully, and American business in large volume continued to be transacted at Lloyd's.

Developments to 1951

Non-marine insurance posed difficulties for the Lloyd's system. As has been explained earlier, it had developed in the nineteenth-century. Lloyd's was well adapted to cope with marine insurance, which is primarily the insurance of property, namely ships and cargo, with a stated value. There were many knowledgeable underwriters, each of whom was prepared to risk a limited sum on most such insurances. Fire insurance is also mainly property insurance and the same system could be applied to it, but much twentieth-century non-marine insurance is liability insurance. In such insurances quite a small premium can involve a possible liability of hundreds of thousands of pounds. It is inconvenient to spread the business among a large number of underwriting syndicates, each of which could accept only a fraction. And the number of active underwriters with a knowledge of the many varieties of non-marine business was small. Hence a tendency arose for syndicates to grow in size, so that too many did not have to be involved in any given insurance. In 1865 most syndicates had no more than three members and the maximum tended to be six. In 1890 a syndicate with ten members was still exceptional. By 1952 there were sixteen syndicates of 100 members or more, the biggest having more than 300. Large syndicates were found particularly necessary for motor insurance. An organisation comparable to that of an insurance company was needed to cope with constant changes to policies and with the frequent claims which could arise in any part of the country. Even so, Lloyd's was not very successful in competing for motor insurance. The largest syndicate (the White Cross) was bought by an insurance company in 1917. By 1950, when the insurance companies transacted £100 million of motor business, Lloyd's had less than £5 million of it.

Larger syndicates meant that there was much work to do in finding new members, in managing their affairs, and in running the syndicates, each of which operated much as an insurance company in its own right. Some active underwriters managed their own syndicates. Others relied for management on insurance brokers, who tended to have bigger staffs than underwriters.

Underwriting agencies were at first partnerships, but in the 1930s limited liability companies began to be admitted as agents. Of the first six of these, five were companies that also transacted insurance broking. They were known as broker-agents.

Although active underwriters were a distinct species from brokers there was a mixture of roles. Enterprising underwriters would form broking firms to get business or to place their reinsurances. The directors of a broking company were likely themselves to be Names, as underwriting members of Lloyd's are called. Brokers were often given binding authorities, known as binders, to grant cover for a given class of insurance to specified classes of prospective insured.

By 1951 Lloyd's premium income was £195 million. The number of underwriting members was rising by 100 or so each year and had reached 2,913. Of the 286 syndicates, there were 150 marine, 100 non-marine, 14 aviation, 21 motor and 1 transacting life insurance. There were 228 Lloyd's brokers. Their number was static.

In the twentieth-century a number of market associations were formed at Lloyd's to discuss and deal with problems arising in various markets. An association of marine underwriters in 1909 was followed by one for fire and non-marine underwriters in 1910. The Lloyd's Motor Underwriters' Association dates from 1931. An aviation underwriters' association began in 1935 with three members. The Lloyd's Insurance Brokers' Association was set up in 1910.

The central services provided by the committee of Lloyd's are described in Chapter 10. Most of them originated between 1850 and 1951. As these services grew so did the central staff of Lloyd's, putting pressure on the space available at the Royal Exchange, which remained the home of Lloyd's until 1928. In that year Lloyd's moved into a home of its own, built for it in Leadenhall Street. In 1936 Lloyd's acquired the freehold both of its site and of the adjacent Royal Mail House. Pressure of staff numbers again built up and in 1959 Lloyd's acquired the freehold of an adjacent site in Lime Street on which the present Lloyd's building stands. For a time it seemed as if the problem of accommodation had been solved once and for all – but the pace of development was quickening.

CHAPTER FOUR

LLOYD'S SINCE 1952

As the Red Queen said to Alice, 'It takes all the running you can do, to keep in the same place. If you want to get somewhere else you must run at least twice as fast as that!' During the past thirty years Lloyd's has expanded at an unprecedented rate, but world insurance has expanded even more, so that Lloyd's share of total premiums for general insurance has fallen. Lloyd's has had a hard task to adapt its organisation to the modern world. On the whole it has succeeded, but not without the occasional stumble.

Changes in market structure

Demand for insurance has grown in two main ways. First, the spread of car ownership in the world has meant that in many countries motor insurance has become the largest class of general insurance. To obtain its share of the United Kingdom's motor insurance business (about one-fifth) Lloyd's underwriters were forced to modify their practice of dealing only with Lloyd's brokers. In 1965 it was agreed that motor insurance syndicates might correspond directly with other brokers, provided that a Lloyd's broker acted as sponsor for them. The motor syndicates had to expand their membership to cope with the increasing flow of business. The number of motor syndicates, twenty-one in 1952, reached forty-six in 1981.

Second, the process of merging in the industrial and financial world meant that much property came into the hands of multinational and other very large corporations whose insurance needs differed from those of smaller companies. They could cope from their own resources with quite substantial losses, but they needed protection against catastrophes. Many large organisations formed their own captive insurance companies to deal with their run-of-the-mill risks. In seeking insurance advice they looked to large brokers with international knowledge and connections and a range of technical expertise. When an industrial merger took place the brokers of the smaller company that was being merged tended to lose their business to the brokers of the parent company. Medium-sized brokers, faced with the loss of important clients, often had to throw in their lot with larger brokers. In the 1970s even the largest British brokers found themselves liable to take-over by the still larger American mega-brokers, as happened to the Bowring Group in 1980 and Alexander Howden in 1982. Although new companies have frequently been formed by individuals breaking away from old ones, the concentration of broking business has continued. In 1951 there were 228 Lloyd's brokers, in 1981, 270, but those 270 represented no more than 166 groups. Many Lloyd's brokers are quite small. It is the number of medium-sized brokers that has declined. In 1978 two-fifths of the business at Lloyd's was placed by three broker-groups and two-thirds by the largest twelve groups.

The demand for insurance cover in large lumps has led to an increase in the size of underwriting syndicates. Some have more than a thousand Names on them. There were 288 syndicates in 1952, and 423 in 1981. The increase in number has been greatest in non-marine (from 99 to 159) and in aviation (from 15 to 52).

Another change has been in the shift from direct insurance to reinsurance. Many countries have either set up government insurance or reinsurance corporations with monopoly powers or have otherwise prohibited or restricted the right to insure outside their borders. Business that would have reached Lloyd's as direct insurance now comes by way of reinsurance from overseas government insurance corporations or from private insurance companies. Similarly the captive insurance companies owned by large industries reinsure extensively at Lloyd's. Insurance brokers have formed reinsurance broking subsidiaries.

Despite all the changes in the structure of the market Lloyd's underwriters have been remarkably successful in underwriting profitability. Figure 4.1 shows their record for 1952-1979. The only unprofitable years for Lloyd's as a whole were 1965-1967, though, of course, many individual syndicates have often sustained losses.

Economists speak of the insurance cycle. They point out that the supply of insurance can be easily expanded by the entry into the market of more capital. When supply increases faster than demand, premium rates are liable to be forced down by competition to the point of unprofitability and even below that point. Sooner or later the weaker units will leave the market, the balance between supply and demand will be restored and premium rates can be raised again to a profitable level.

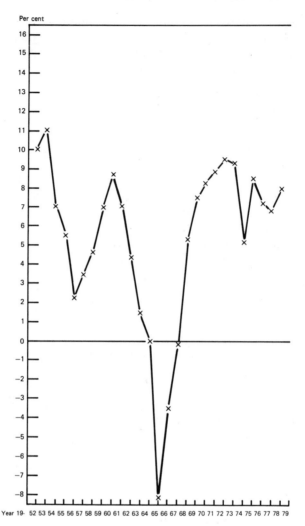

Figure 4.1 Lloyd's Balances on Global Underwriting Accounts 1952–1979

Source – Lloyd's

The cycle then repeats itself. It used to be thought that the cycle for general insurance was one of five to seven years. In the more distant past when the demand for insurance remained comparatively static over a period, or even, in the case of marine insurance, fell, the operation of the cycle could be clearly seen. In modern times, with the expansion of the world economy and consequently a rise year by year in the demand for insurance, the cycle is less obvious. Since World War II demand has been rising and in the late 1960s voices were heard to suggest that the supply of insurance had become inadequate for world needs. The demand, it was said, was growing at the rate of 10 per cent per annum. At Lloyd's capital for underwriting could only come from Names. Between 1952 and 1968 the number of Names had not quite doubled. There were 3,157 in 1952 and 6,059 in 1968. The number of new applicants was falling rather than rising at that time, because of the unfavourable underwriting results for 1965 that had just been announced. Lloyd's first step to counteract the falling tendency was to offer to admit nationals of countries outside the Commonwealth. This took effect in 1969. In that year the Committee decided that it would in 1970 admit to membership British women domiciled in the United Kingdom. A year later it agreed to admit women of any nationality.

Changes in underwriting

Underwriting has on occasion posed special problems in the past thirty years. Lloyd's in general operates on the principle that what is not prohibited is permissible, but there are situations in which the insurance of certain risks, while not unlawful, is considered politically undesirable. In 1952 the underwriter Sir Eustace Pulbrook, a former Chairman of Lloyd's, insured Liberal candidates against the loss of their deposits at a general election. (A candidate lost his deposit if he received less than one-eighth of the total votes cast.) The Liberals had a pretty disastrous experience. Since then such insurances have been impermissible in case they should be considered contrary to public policy. Similarly insurances against the effect of strikes by an employer's own workforce, or by a trade union against a loss of its members' earnings during a strike, are regarded as impermissible. A more debatable case is that of kidnap and ransom insurance. It could be argued that such insurance, which offers to pay ransom money, is undesirable because it operates for the benefit of the criminals concerned. Indeed, if the existence of an insurance is known it could be an encouragement to kidnappers. Some states, notably Italy, have forbidden it, but kidnap and ransom insurance is commonly accepted at Lloyd's and indeed has grown to sizeable proportions. Precautions that underwriters can take include forbidding the insured to disclose the existence of the insurance and requiring him to meet the cost of ransom out of his own resources before he becomes entitled to claim an indemnity. In recent years a number of insurance companies, including some large American ones, have followed Lloyd's into the kidnap and ransom insurance market as there is a strong demand for it from multinational companies operating in countries where the risk is high.

The comparatively even tenor of underwriting has been twice subject to a violent upset during the last thirty years. Both upsets came from the United States. The hurricanes of the early 1960s, coupled with other factors, led to almost unprecedented underwriting losses in 1963–1965. In 1976 there were also commercial problems for Lloyd's, arising from the transaction of computer leasing insurance in the United States. This form of insurance indemnified companies leasing computers against losses arising on the termination of leasing contracts. In the normal course of events it was expected that the computers reverting to the companies would have a high value, but the advent of a new generation of cheap computers led to the wholesale termination of leases at a time when the returned computers proved to be of little value. Claims assumed serious proportions. The estimate of claims made against all insurers rose progressively to US $444 million by November 1981, of which Lloyd's share would, it was thought, be upwards of £150 million. In the event the market had little difficulty in absorbing the losses, though some underwriters, with the benefit of hindsight, admitted that it was unwise to have written the business without a full appreciation of the speed of technological change affecting the value of old computers.

Expansion in administrative services

Throughout the last thirty years the Corporation of Lloyd's has had to expand and rationalise the services it offers to the market. Until 1961 underwriters were supplied by Lloyd's Policy Signing Office with details of premiums payable and claims due, but settlement took place between each syndicate and each broker. Under the central accounting system introduced in 1961 all money due in account is paid through the central machinery. For the Lloyd's American Trust Fund and the Lloyd's Canadian Trust Fund, which was set up in 1971, the settlement is through the fund concerned. The LPSO processes over 12 million items annually. Lloyd's computer services have been greatly developed for the provision of statistics. Most of this work is now carried on at Lloyd's new office at Gun Wharf, Chatham, which was officially opened in 1979. Among the departments housed there are the LPSO, the Accounts, Membership, Management Service, Personnel and Training Departments, with some 800 staff in all.

An integrated claims and recovery service for marine underwriters was set up in 1977 by the amalgamation of the Lloyd's Underwriters' Claims Office and the Average and Recoveries Department. It is now used by the majority of underwriters for claims under both direct insurance and reinsurance.

Lloyd's printing and publishing services were reorganised and hived off into a separate company, Lloyd's of London Press Limited, which was formed in 1973. Two years later the printing department moved to Colchester, from where the company operates with about 200 staff.

A number of new departments have had to be formed in the past thirty

The exterior of Lloyd's Coffee House, 1808. Lloyd's was developing into a national institution, but even today its Coffee House origins survive through many traditions.

photo: courtesy of Lloyd's

A caricature of the Coffee Room at Lloyd's in the Royal Exchange, 1798. Rooms were leased in the Royal Exchange in 1773, due to the overcrowding of the Coffee House in Pope's Head Alley. *photo: courtesy of Lloyd's*

The 1838 fire that destroyed the first Royal Exchange. It burnt many of Lloyd's records and forced them to move for a while to Threadneadle Street.

photo: courtesy of Lloyd's

The new Royal Exchange, rebuilt in 1844. It was about this time that strict rules began to be made regarding underwriting membership of Lloyd's.

photo: courtesy of Lloyd's

The present Lloyd's building in Lime Street, opened by the Queen in 1957. It had 44,250 square feet, but it was only a matter of time before Lloyd's was forced to commission an even bigger building.   *photo: courtesy of Lloyd's*

An architect's model of the Lloyd's building presently under construction in Leadenhall Street. Due to be completed in 1985, it has 95,000 square feet and is planned to provide enough room for the next fifty years.

years. One example is the Training Department, which not only provides training for the Corporation's own staff, but also runs courses for the benefit of all who work in the Lloyd's market.

Successive moves

The pressure on space at Lloyd's has mounted inexorably. When Lloyd's moved to its new building in Leadenhall Street in 1928 people must have thought that the problem of accommodation had been solved for good. By 1948 expansion meant that the need for space was as pressing as ever. Lloyd's had to go into the property market again. In 1952 the Queen laid the foundation of a new building in Lime Street which opened in 1957. The accommodation was planned to be adequate for the rest of the century, but once again the plan was to prove over-optimistic.

Terence Heysham was the architect of the 1957 building. It provided 44,250 square feet for the underwriting room, with a gallery on all sides. Two rooms are especially noteworthy. The Nelson Room, off the under-writing room, houses many treasures relating to Nelson and the wars he fought in, including Nelson's sword, a log book containing his famous signal at Trafalgar, and quantities of silver presented by Lloyd's to Nelson and other naval officers of his time, which Lloyd's has since re-acquired. Another notable room is the Committee Room, adapted from the Adam Great Room of Bowood House, Wiltshire, with an Adam ceiling and chimney-piece and three great chandeliers.

By 1970 Lloyd's was in desperate need of further space. Step by step the galleries have been filled with underwriters' boxes. Boxes have even spread to the basement, known as the 'Yellow Submarine'. Half of Lloyd's central staff has been dispersed to Colchester and Chatham. Many others remaining in London have had to occupy outside premises in Fenchurch Street. In 1979 the Committee again took the plunge when it commissioned Richard Rogers, architect of the Pompidou Centre in Paris, to build a new headquarters side by side with its 1957 building. This has involved the demolition of the Leadenhall Street building, except for the ceremonial arch fronting on Leadenhall Street. The new building will have translucent glass panels offset by vertical structural columns with a silver-grey metallic finish and with six service towers clad in aluminium and glass. It will stand in a sunken landscaped concourse. The initial underwriting space is expected to be 95,000 square feet on the main floor as well as two galleries with scope for expansion to four further galleries if necessary. It is expected that the new building, due for completion in 1985, will suffice for the next fifty years.

The Cromer Report

In 1968 the Committee of Lloyd's appointed a working party of seven chaired by Lord Cromer, former Governor of the Bank of England, with Sir Alexander Johnston who had been chairman of the Board of Inland Revenue, Sir Alexander Cairncross, head of the Government Economics Department, and four members of the Committee of Lloyd's. Its terms of reference were to recommend what steps should be taken to encourage and maintain an efficient and profitable Lloyd's market of independent competing syndicates which would be of a size to command world attention. Lloyd's did not publish the Working Party's report, but issued a summary in 1970.

The Cromer Report concluded that although a small select spread of risks might seem safe, Lloyd's would lose if people believed that it could not or would not underwrite large-scale risks or that rates were too high. The capacity of the market was inextricably bound up with profitability which largely depended on the technical skill of underwriters. Lloyd's needed a steadily increasing amount of capital. The number of people eligible for membership of Lloyd's was not falling, but a restoration of profitability was essential to attract new applicants.

The report proposed a simplification of the requirements for a show of means, which at that time varied for relatives of Lloyd's Names, commercial Names and unconnected non-commercial Names. For the last mentioned category the report recommended that there should be a reduction from £75,000 to £50,000, while foreign Names should be admitted on showing means of £75,000 instead of £100,000. The means test needed to be a continuous requirement. The report also recommended that persons at Lloyd's continue to be admitted as Names without a show of means unless they wanted to write higher amounts of premiums, in which case they must show means of at least £25,000. These proposals were accepted, as was another suggestion that Lloyd's deposits and the Premiums Trust Fund deposit should be amalgamated and held on behalf of members by the committee of Lloyd's. The Committee agreed to a simplification in the calculation of premium limits based on a fuller use of members' deposited resources.

The report affirmed that unlimited liability on the part of members should remain a Lloyd's principle, but it also proposed that limited companies should be allowed to become members. This recommendation was made subject to a number of limitations: the company must be a United Kingdom company with a paid-up capital of at least £1 million; brokers, insurance companies and companies specially formed for the purpose of underwriting would be excluded; and company participation in any syndicate would be limited to 10 per cent. The recommendation was considered, but not adopted. If carried out it would have entailed a fundamental alteration in the operation of Lloyd's, with a consequent re-opening of settled tax practices and a need for new legislation.

The report pointed out that at times there was a surplus of capacity in one of the main markets at Lloyd's and a shortage of capacity in another. It recommended greater flexibility. The marine market, for example, had been allowed to write some so-called 'incidental' non-marine business. Why should not the converse apply to the non-marine market?

It was calculated that if Lloyd's adopted all the various measures proposed, existing underwriters could increase their capacity by £100 million. In the event, not only was capacity increased in various ways, but an influx of new members entered Lloyd's, so that by the end of the 1970s Lloyd's was beginning to doubt whether all its capacity could be utilised.

Among other reforms resulting from the Cromer Report were a simplification of the rules governing the extent of reinsurance permitted in the calculation of premium limits, and new by-laws regularising the authorisation of underwriting agencies.

The combined effects of widening eligibility for membership and implementing parts of the Cromer Report meant that in ten years the underwriting membership of Lloyd's trebled, from 6,020 in 1971 to 19,136 in 1981. We hear no more talk of lack of capacity. Some syndicates have found it difficult to transact enough insurance to fill their premium quotas, though some, on the other hand, have written more premiums than they were entitled to write.

Recent difficulties

It is inevitable that in a free market some individuals will transgress against the rules, whether inadvertently or deliberately. No system of regulation can be fully proofed against criminal activity. A bad example arose in 1954 when A. E. M. Wilcox, a broker and underwriting agent, became insolvent. It was found that for some years the underwriting accounts had been falsified in connivance with the chartered accountant responsible for the audit. Both Wilcox and the accountant went to prison. The Committee of Lloyd's, exceptionally, provided money to relieve Wilcox's innocent Names of their normal underwriting liability. All policyholders' claims were met so the public was not hurt. Insolvencies among insurance companies were a feature of the early 1970s. They led to the Policyholders Protection Act 1975, which required solvent insurance companies to pay by means of a levy the claims of any United Kingdom policyholders which could not be met by an insolvent insurance company. The Act excluded Lloyd's from its operation because Lloyd's security, including its Central Reserve Fund, was thought to be protection enough for Lloyd's policyholders.

In recent years, a number of incidents have occurred which have led to public criticism of Lloyd's way of business and its system of internal regulation.

One dispute at Lloyd's which dragged on for some time and attracted considerable publicity was the *Savonita* affair. In November 1974 a cargo of cars owned by Fiat was damaged by fire when aboard the *Savonita*. The cargo was insured by SIAT, an Italian insurance company controlled by the parent company of Fiat. A director of Willis, Faber & Dumas (WFD), one of the largest Lloyd's brokers, was a director of SIAT. SIAT's reinsurance of the bulk of the *Savonita* risk had been placed at Lloyd's by Pearson, Webb and Springbett (PWS), a comparatively small Lloyd's broker. SIAT settled the claim for the damaged cars on payment of the insured value less 15 per cent, said to be the value of the cars after the fire, and PWS presented a claim of $711.643 on their behalf to the Lloyd's underwriters under the reinsurance. A few months later PWS concluded that the claim was inflated as the salvage was worth more than had been allowed in its calculation. The leading Lloyd's underwriter offered full settlement, but PWS refused to accept and invited him to ask for further details. The underwriters accordingly appointed an adjuster to investigate further on their behalf. He confirmed PWS's impression that the claim was grossly inflated. SIAT subsequently dismissed PWS as their brokers and appointed WFD in their stead with a mandate to collect the claim. The reinsurance agreement provided that the reinsurers must 'follow all settlements' by the company they reinsured and the reinsurers were legally advised that they would probably fail if they sought to contest SIAT's claim. Three years after the fire WFD succeeded in recovering from them a large proportion of the claim. In the opinion of PWS, WFD had exercised undue pressure on the underwriters. The underwriters denied this, but PWS's dissatisfaction remained and an MP raised the matter in the House of Commons on 23 March 1978.

The Committee of Lloyd's appointed a Board of Inquiry which concluded that WFD's presentation of the claim had been 'robust beyond the normally accepted standards of broking conduct'. At the same time the Board of Inquiry questioned PWS's conduct in handling the claim. They should either have pursued it, the Board concluded, or have informed their clients that they were not prepared to act.

A curious situation arose. While Lloyd's was telling journalists that the Board's report was confidential, it was published in full in *Lloyd's List* of 8 December 1978. As has been seen, the report contained nothing unsavoury about Lloyd's, but the whole affair demonstrated the conflicts that can arise in an institution made up of units that compete strongly among themselves. In a monolithic organisation these conflicts would not become public.

The affairs of the Sasse syndicate brought to public attention problems inherent in the Lloyd's system. Turnbull Sasse was the underwriting agent for non-marine syndicate number 762. The syndicate included some members introduced to it by other underwriting agents, so that

Turnbull Sasse was only a sub-agent for those members. It conducted a mixed non-marine account which included fire and leasing insurance. Early in 1976 the underwriter, Mr F. H. (Tim) Sasse gave a binding authority to Den-Har Underwriters in the United States which enabled Den-Har to give cover on property in city ghetto areas. Den-Har wrote a large volume of such business at low rates and although its authority was soon cancelled, claims began to flow in. By December 1976 it was apparent to Lloyd's that the syndicate had largely exceeded its premium limits, but its underwriting was allowed to continue and further losses were incurred until its suspension on 29 December 1977. Its affairs were then put in the hands of Merrett Dixey, another firm of underwriting agents, as caretaker managers.

The Names on the Sasse syndicate were shocked at the extent of their potential losses, all the more because the syndicate's reinsurers, including the IRB (the Brazilian reinsurance institution) and another Lloyd's syndicate, were resisting claims under reinsurance contracts on the ground that they had not been informed of material facts about the business they had undertaken to reinsure. The Names not unnaturally sought to find someone whom they might make legally responsible for the *débâcle*. Two separate sets of them instituted legal proceedings which involved, among others, the Committee of Lloyd's, Merrett Dixey, and Brentnall Beard, the insurance brokers who had introduced Den-Har. Many interesting points of law arose, notably over the binding authority given by Mr Sasse to Den-Har. There was a procedure whereby Lloyd's Non-marine Underwriters' Association was supposed to 'tribunalise' or, in other words, investigate and approve, the person to whom a binding authority was to be granted but this procedure had not been followed in the case of Den-Har. The Names also pointed out that the Lloyd's Act 1871 expressed as a 'fundamental rule' (rule 3) that 'All underwriting business at Lloyd's shall be conducted in the underwriting rooms, and not elsewhere.' This provision was, they said, breached by the issue of a binding authority to someone outside Lloyd's, giving him power to underwrite. Those members whose underwriting agents had employed Turnbull Sasse as sub-agents also claimed that under the law of agency sub-agents are not empowered to delegate their duties to another sub-agent. They complained too that the Committee of Lloyd's had insisted on the implementation of insurances issued under the binding authority, though they might have been legally voidable.

Not all the Names could conveniently meet their liabilities. In April 1979, in order that Lloyd's should be able to satisfy audit requirements for the purpose of Department of Trade returns, the Committee agreed to issue letters of credits for up to £7 million to help the Names to borrow money, but even so the audit deadline had to be extended. In the course of 1979 Merrett Dixey felt unable to continue with work for the Sasse syndicate and the Committee had to form a company to take the work over, acting at arm's length from the Committee.

Finally, at a meeting of underwriting agents and leading underwriters in July 1980, the market agreed to relieve the Names (except those actively concerned with the underwriting) by limiting their liability for 1976 to £6.25 million and putting them in a 'no loss' situation for 1977. The syndicate's excess of liability was met by a levy of 0.3 per cent on the 1981 premium income of all who were Names in 1980. Some underwriters felt that this was an undesirable precedent for relieving Names of the consequences of their unfortunate choice of underwriting agent, but there was general relief that the running sore of the Sasse affair had been remedied. In the sequel substantial reinsurance recoveries were made, notably from the IRB. In 1982 people connected with Den-Har went to prison in New York, either for conspiracy to make away with the premiums or, in the case of Dennis Harrison, after whom Den-Har was named, for tax offences.

Other troubles were besetting Lloyd's in these years. In 1979 three syndicates managed by Ashby and Co. voluntarily suspended operations. Besides this, Lloyd's broker Mr Christopher Moran was the subject of criticisms which led him to sue the *Daily Telegraph* for defamation. The action failed. He and an underwriter were subsequently prosecuted for conspiracy to defraud. The case lingered on for a year before they were found not guilty.

The Committee of Lloyd's brought into play its disciplinary procedure dating from 1871 against Mr Moran and Mr Reid Wilson, an active underwriter to Mr Moran's syndicate number 566. At an arbitration hearing a tribunal had found Mr Moran guilty of acts and defaults discreditable to him in connection with the business of insurance. A special general meeting of Lloyd's on 28 October 1982 voted by the requisite 80 per cent majority to expel Mr Moran, but a motion to expel Mr Wilson failed as the majority for expulsion (957 against 610) was less than 80 per cent.

Some of the most important of recent difficulties have arisen in connection with the Alexander Howden Group (AHG), comprising one of the largest Lloyd's brokers and one of the largest underwriting agencies, Alexander Howden Underwriting (AHU). Among the Group's directors was Mr Ian Posgate who was both the leading underwriter for AHU and for another underwriting agency, Posgate & Denby Agencies (P & D). Mr Posgate was reputed to be the highest paid underwriter at Lloyd's, with remuneration in 1981 of over £350,000. He had been elected to the Committee of Lloyd's for 1982. His underwriting activities were on a very large scale; two of his syndicates had a membership of 3,800.

In January 1982 Alexander & Alexander (A & A), the United States insurance brokers, acquired the AHG and commissioned accountants to conduct a 'fair value audit'. Arising out of this the AHG reported to the Chairman of Lloyd's in June 1982 that AHU had been instructed to write no more 1982 business because they were concerned about over-writing, that is, exceeding the premium limits allocated to each syndicate. The Committee of Lloyd's, which had already been monitoring AHU syndicates by means of quarterly returns because of earlier over-writing, instructed accountants to examine the affairs of AHU.

In September 1982, Mr Bogardus, the Chairman of A & A, informed the Chairman of Lloyd's that the board of A & A was proposing to remove Mr Posgate as an underwriter for, and a director of, AHU. The Committee of Lloyd's thereupon informed AHU and P & D that if they were not to lose approval as underwriting agents they must suspend Mr Posgate as active underwriter and director and suspend underwriting until the Committee satisfied itself as to their underwriting capability and financial position; AHU and P & D complied.

Mr Posgate asked the court for a judicial review of the Committee's action in requiring his suspension. The court held that the Committee had no power to require the suspension of Mr Posgate in such manner as would amount to suspending him as a member of Lloyd's and that in any case as a matter of natural justice, Mr Posgate should have been told of the charges against him and asked if he had grounds for saying that it would be wrong to suspend him.

By the time the judgment was given on 11 January 1983, the Lloyd's Act 1982 had established a Council of Lloyd's with new powers, one of which it immediately exercised by passing a by-law which enabled it to suspend any member. On 17 January the Council notified Mr Posgate that it was considering the issue of a direction to suspend him and that he had a right to make representations to a sub-committee. He exercised that right, but was nonetheless suspended.

A & A had meanwhile been alleging that Posgate and four former directors of the AHG, including its ex-Chairman, had been involved in fraudulent transactions whereby reinsurance premiums had been paid to companies in which they had an interest that had not been disclosed. A & A had taken legal proceedings against those concerned. Mr Posgate, who stoutly resisted allegations of fraud, sued A & A for wrongful dismissal. Litigation on his behalf was also under contemplation against the Council of Lloyd's. In a separate incident Mr Peter Brewis, the former Deputy Chairman of Alexander Howden Insurance Brokers and an annual subscriber to Lloyd's, was suspended for fourteen months on the strength of a misstatement he was alleged to have made when successfully tendering for the insurance of the Qantas Airline in competition with another broker.

Late in 1982, Mr John Wallrock, Chairman of another large Lloyd's broker, J. H. Minet, resigned after admitting that some US $40 million

had been channelled to off-shore reinsurance companies in Liechten-
stein, Gibraltar and Guernsey in which he had a personal interest. Both
the Department of Trade and the Committee of Lloyd's instituted
inquiries into the AHG and Minet Holdings. Another underwriting
agency, PCW (Underwriting Agencies) Ltd sued Mr P. S. Dixon, who
controlled its shareholders and directors, alleging that a secret profit had
been made out of reinsurances with companies in Gibraltar in which he
had a financial interest. Lloyd's also instituted an inquiry into reinsurances of syndicates number 89 and 880 managed by Brookgate
Underwriting Agencies and said to have been placed in part with
Fidentia Marine Insurance, a Bermuda-based insurance company.

There have been other incidents too resulting in suspensions. The
point should be made that while the numerous recent incidents have
brought into question the integrity of some members of the Lloyd's
community, they concern only the internal working of Lloyd's. No
policyholder has been in jeopardy of failing to recover whatever is due to
him under a Lloyd's policy. On the other hand the happenings have
highlighted the risks run by Names, with their unlimited liability if
anything goes wrong in the conduct of the syndicates to which they
belong.

As a sequel to the Sasse and other incidents at the time, the Committee
of Lloyd's in 1980 appointed the Fisher Working Party. Its report, and
consequences that led to the Lloyd's Act 1982, will be described in
Chapter 9.

CHAPTER FIVE

THE MEMBERSHIP

In 1982 Lloyd's had 20,145 members. Nearly nine-tenths were United Kingdom and Commonwealth citizens residing in the United Kingdom. Overseas members were not admitted until 1969. Sixty countries were represented in the membership, with the United States having by far the largest share at 1,370 members. The Republic of Ireland and South Africa had the next largest contingents (232 each), followed by Australia (222), Canada (187) and New Zealand (100). No other country had as many as fifty. Japan had only one, as had China, Romania and Yugoslavia. A fuller distribution is shown in Table 5.1.

The turnover of members is small. In 1982, for example, only 137 members were reported to have resigned, while 161 died.

By opening the membership to all countries in 1969 Lloyd's met a growing demand from the United States and the European Economic Community and at the same time gave itself the prospect of broadening its capital base. The doors were opened to women in 1970. Now 3,890 women are members, of whom 3,575 are United Kingdom or Commonwealth citizens, most of the rest coming from the United States. It has become quite common for wives to join husbands in the membership. A more cautious view would be that a wife with the requisite means should take up her own membership rather than that of her husband, so that there is no risk of the solvency of both being impaired at the same time.

The membership comprises a cross-section of wealthy people. It includes, besides businessmen, many peers and others with inherited wealth, two past prime ministers, scores of MPs, entertainers and sports people who have taken financial advice on the management of their funds, such as Henry Cooper, Lester Piggott and Virginia Wade.

Table 5.1 Distribution of Membership at 1 January 1982

		Members	Per cent
United Kingdom		17,393	86.6
Commonwealth			
(including United Kingdom residents)			
Australia	222		
Canada	187		
New Zealand	100		
Other	62	571	2.8
European Community			
Republic of Ireland	232		
France	47		
Belgium	40		
West Germany	34		
Netherlands	29		
Italy	20		
Greece	17		
Denmark	13	432	2.1
United States		1,370	6.7
South Africa		232	1.1
Rest of the world		147	0.7
		20,145	100.0

Source – Lloyd's

The point of membership is that it entitles the member to have insurances written at Lloyd's on his behalf and at his risk. Lloyd's members provide all the capital on which insurances at Lloyd's are based. To that extent members are comparable to the shareholders in any insurance company, but there is an important difference. In any insurance company the shareholder's liability is limited to the value of his shares. At Lloyd's if the business written on behalf of a member shows a loss, the member is personally liable without limit of amount.

Applying for membership

An applicant for membership must be aged twenty-one or over and sponsored by a member of Lloyd's to whom he (or she) is well known. Applications are submitted through an underwriting agent. The applicant from outside Lloyd's must show that he has a stated minimum of means in readily realisable assets. Readily realisable assets are divided into two categories. Sixty per cent must be in the first category. This comprises Stock Exchange quoted securities, cash at a bank or building society, the surrender value of life policies, absolute reversionary interests in trusts (taken at market value and calculated on an actuarial basis), gold at 70 per cent of market value and irrevocable bank guarantees or letters of credit. Neither gold nor the value of any one Stock Exchange security may count for more than 30 per cent of the total means.

The remaining 40 per cent may be satisfied by landed property and certain leaseholds net of any mortgages or loans on them and not including the first £50,000 of the value of the member's residence.

It will be seen that assets that are not readily realisable do not count. These, including cars, yachts, jewellery or the applicant's own house, do not count unless they are the subject of a bank guarantee or letter of credit.

The statement of means must be signed by the applicant, an approved bank with a branch in the United Kingdom, or a firm of United Kingdom solicitors or accountants, or associated firms of the latter. The means test is a continuing requirement. The applicant for underwriting membership is required to confirm his means every four years and to notify the Committee if his means fall below the required level at any time.

The extent to which insurance may be undertaken on behalf of the applicant when he is admitted to membership is governed by a combination of the means disclosed and the amount deposited.

In general the minimum net worth that must be shown is £100,000 for British citizens and citizens of the Commonwealth or the European Economic Community and £135,000 for others. A lower means test of £50,000 is, however, available to British citizens or Commonwealth or European Economic Community citizens if resident and domiciled in the United Kingdom. The premium income to be written on behalf of a member must not exceed double his net worth.

Once the means test has been passed, if the application appears to be in order the applicant is asked to travel to London for an interview with members of the Committee who form a sub-committee known as the Rota Committee. The Rota Committee is required to satisfy itself that the applicant knows the risk involved in membership which may result in unlimited liability and that he appreciates the nature of membership, in that there is no guaranteed return on a member's investment. The applicant is encouraged to meet the active underwriters of the syndicates he contemplates joining as shown in the application. At one time the Rota Committee conducted an individual interview with every applicant. Nowadays ten or twelve are interviewed in a group.

Applications have to be made early in the calendar year before admission is sought, as all members are admitted from 1 January. The applicant's name is posted in the Room so that any member may raise an objection to the proposed election.

Persons accepted for membership are required to give a 'general undertaking' to the Committee. Among other things the member agrees to place premiums received in trust, to submit his accounts to an annual audit, and to provide information about his underwriting when required. He also undertakes to observe market agreements (*see* Chapter 11) and to submit disputes to arbitration. He assents to various aspects of Lloyd's practice, such as the policy signing procedure and the ban on writing financial guarantee business. He undertakes that if his means are not maintained he will inform the Committee. The undertaking on this last point was introduced for new members in 1971 and strengthened in 1978. Members entering before 1971 are therefore not subject to it. In 1981, however, a procedure whereby means have to be confirmed every four years was instituted.

In accordance with recommendations in the Fisher Report of 1980 it is to be expected that the obligations of members will in future be set out in by-laws or regulations applicable to all members.

Working Names

One special category of members consists of so-called Lloyd's Names, also called Working Names. For these the means test is not applied. The category is confined to persons who have worked actively and continuously in the business of Lloyd's for five years with a Lloyd's broker or underwriting agent. They must be earning at least £10,000 a year and be supported in their application by their employer. The five year period may in special cases be reduced, as where an applicant becomes an active underwriter. The maximum premium that a Lloyd's Name is permitted to write is £50,000 and the deposit ratio is 35 per cent. Lloyd's Names comprised 12 per cent of the membership in 1980 and accounted for 4 per cent of Lloyd's premiums capacity.

The system of making special provision for those who work at Lloyd's is praiseworthy in that it attracts ambitious young people to Lloyd's and helps them to further their career, but it is open to criticism in that a Lloyd's Name without substantial means may be exposed to loss he can ill afford. His employer may, or may not, fund the loss. If it is heavy, repaying it may constitute a burden for years. Even where the Lloyd's Name believes that support is available it may be lost through the death of the supporter or through a concern going out of business. It has been suggested that at times an employee has been put under pressure to become a Lloyd's Name despite reluctance to assume the potential liability that that course entails.

Members' fees and deposits

Once a member has been elected the entrance fee becomes payable. It varies according to the category of membership. The maximum is £2,000.

For taxation purposes it is treated as a capital payment. It is not refundable and is expressed as a percentage (currently 0.55 per cent or 0.6 per cent) of the allocated premium limit.

The allocated premium limit will indicate the deposit to be made. Within the maximum allowable as indicated by his means, it will be proportionate to the deposit he chooses to make. The proportion depends on the nationality, domicile and residence of the member. For a member who is a United Kingdom Commonwealth or European Economic Community citizen domiciled and resident in the United Kingdom, the deposit is 25 per cent of the premium limit, with a minimum of £12,500. Thus, someone whose means are £150,000 and who wants a premium limit of the maximum he can take, namely £300,000, the deposit will be £75,000. For a United Kingdom, Commonwealth or European Economic Community citizen domiciled outside the United Kingdom, the deposit will be at the rate of 30 per cent, that is, £90,000. For a foreign national, who is not a Commonwealth or European Economic community citizen, the minimum deposit is £26,000 and the rate is 35 per cent, so the deposit required would be £105,000.

Deposits may be (and in the case of the last mentioned category, must as a rule be) in the form of letters of credit or bank guarantees. Where investments are deposited, a minimum of 25 per cent must be in cash or short-dated British government stock. For members in the United Kingdom, as an alternative to a deposit, the Committee will accept a guarantee from an approved life assurance company to provide cash up to a predetermined level out of the proceeds of annuities or endowment assurances effected by the member.

Where investments are deposited they are held in trust for the discharge of the member's underwriting liabilities. The income on them goes to the member. With the permission of the Committee of Lloyd's he may change the underlying securities from time to time. He may increase his deposit at the outset of any year if he wishes to increase his premium limit and can pass the means test required for the higher limit. But he cannot by reducing his premium limit get any of his deposit back. A return is not made until after his underwriting has ceased and all his liabilities have been run off.

Once the premium limit has been determined its allocation will be made, in multiples of £5,000, among the underwriting syndicates which the member proposes to join on the advice of his underwriting agent. Syndicates sometimes over-run their premium allocation. There are penalties and dangers attached to this. The member may find himself being required to increase his deposit at a time when it is inconvenient for him to do so. It may therefore be prudent not to take up one's whole allocation. On the principle of risk spreading it is common to join a number of syndicates in different parts of the market, for example, one marine syndicate, one aviation, one non-marine and one motor, in varying proportions. A loss in one may be compensated for by a profit in others. Only seldom do all classes of insurance have a bad year at the same time.

Membership and taxation

The advantages of underwriting membership of Lloyd's are twofold. First, the member hopes to make a profit on his underwriting, while at the same time drawing interest or dividends on the money he has deposited. Thus his money is used to double advantage. Second, for anyone who is liable to high personal taxation, as most members are, the possibility arises of mitigating his tax liabilities through membership. It is true that the member renders himself liable to tax in some foreign countries, such as the United States and Canada, for underwriting profits derived from those countries, but double taxation agreements are likely to relieve him of any net additional liability to tax.

Except for Working Names, a Name's income from underwriting is treated for tax purposes as investment income rather than earned income. High-rate income taxpayers are naturally concerned to minimise their taxable income, to defer their liability to pay tax as long as possible and, where possible, to receive gains in the form of capital rather than as income, since capital gains are taxed at the rate of 30 per cent only. British government securities held for more than twelve months are free of tax. Syndicates therefore usually invest their fund of premiums and reserves in short-dated government stocks, with the aim of getting capital appreciation at the cost of accepting lower interest income.

The Lloyd's system of accounting means that profits are not ascertained for tax purposes until after three years have expired. The tax on the profits of the first year's underwriting, whether at basic rate or on capital gains, is therefore payable only three years after the accounting date. Payment of the higher rate tax and investment income surcharge is delayed for an additional six months. In the case of capital transfer tax, after two years of underwriting there is the opportunity of 50 per cent business relief and the tax may be paid by instalments.

A member gets no income tax allowance on his entrance fee to Lloyd's but his annual subscription is allowable. Another means of tax mitigation is for the member to pay money out of his underwriting profits for any closed year into a personal special reserve fund to set against possible future underwriting losses. The amount so transferred, up to £7,000 or 50 per cent of underwriting income (whichever is the less), is subject to basic rate tax only. Underwriting income for this purpose includes not only underwriting profit (before deduction of foreign taxes), but also investment income from the Lloyd's deposit, the premiums trust fund deposit, the special reserve fund and any additional personal underwriting reserves. It is common for members to create such additional reserves, but they do not escape any tax on the money put into them.

Special reserve funds are administered by the member's underwriting agent under a trust deed to which the Corporation of Lloyd's is also a party. The fund must be in approved securities. Approval extends not only to those securities approved for members' deposits, but also to bearer securities and investments in companies incorporated overseas. Investments may be changed, but capital appreciation cannot be withdrawn. Inland Revenue approval is required for any releases from the fund.

The returns of income to the American and Canadian revenue authorities are arranged through Lloyd's.

A member may reduce his risk of loss if a syndicate trades unprofitably by effecting a stop-loss insurance. Under such a contract the insurer, in return for a percentage of the member's premium income, agrees that if the member's losses exceed, say, 90 per cent of premiums, the insurer will reimburse the greater part of the losses between 90 per cent and, say, 120 per cent. The premium is in some cases allowable as a business expense and therefore gives rise to tax relief. As a rule underwriters require a member effecting stop-loss insurance to do so on his business in all the syndicates to which he belongs, rather than select a particular syndicate to cover. A popular scheme is one by which if a loss occurs in one year it is repaid out of profits in subsequent years. Income is thus evened over the years for tax purposes.

Role of the Member's Agent

We have seen that applications for underwriting membership must be submitted through an underwriting agency acting as a Members' Agent. The Members' Agent will carry through the procedure for him, advise him on the allocation of his premium limit and recommend to him which syndicates he should join and how much of his premium limit he should allocate to each syndicate. Often the Members' Agent will also act as Managing Agent for a number of syndicates and the new member will be recommended to join some of these. But it also happens that the agency may be a Members' Agent only or that the member decides to join a syndicate not under his own agent's management. A sub-agency agreement will then be necessary to allow the syndicate concerned to write business on behalf of the member. Where a member's interests extend to more than one syndicate the member is required to appoint a co-ordinating agent to watch over his affairs for the purpose of ensuring as far as possible that his premium limits are not exceeded. If they should be exceeded, as sometimes happens, the member must provide additional security in the form of a special deposit which is usually 50 per cent of the excess premium written. The special deposit must be in the form of cash or a bank guarantee or a letter of credit. It will be kept separate and returned only after the underwriting account has been closed. On the first occasion that the premium limit is exceeded a member may use 50 per cent of the market value of his special reserve, if not earmarked, but he cannot have recourse again to the special reserve until the underwriting account in which the limit was first exceeded has been closed.

A member's relationship with his agent is all-important. He relies on the agent to recommend to him syndicates that have a good chance of making an underwriting profit and to monitor the underwriters' performance. The member himself is expected to leave the underwriting entirely to the active underwriters concerned. The member's role is the passive one of providing the capital on which the underwriting is based. It is not for the member to question the underwriter's judgement or to say that he does not wish the underwriter to accept this or that risk or category of risks. If he is dissatisfied his only remedy is to leave the syndicate after a prescribed period of notice.

For further information on the role of the Member's Agent, *see* Chapter 6.

Returns

In financial terms members must be prepared to wait some years before they see any return on their risk capital. They must lay out some thousands of pounds in the form of entrance fee and annual subscriptions, drawing only the interest on their deposits. Under the three-year accounting system the profit on their first year's underwriting is not determined until the expiry of three years. Before the balance is struck any outstanding risks must be reinsured by what is called 'reinsurance to close', that is to say, part of the premiums received are paid over to cover any potential liabilities in respect of the underwriting year that is being closed. The reinsurance is usually, but not necessarily, effected by paying over the premium for it to an open year underwriting account of the same syndicate. The most common method is to transfer the premium for year one to the oldest open year, namely year two, which is still outstanding, but sometimes the method called 'odds to odds, evens to evens' is adopted. Here a year's business is reinsured into the youngest open year. Thus, year one will be reinsured into year three, year two into year four, and so on. Very rarely reinsurance to close is effected into the year about to open.

Even when (after reinsurance to close has been effected and a favourable underwriting balance has been disclosed) taking into account interest and capital appreciation on the syndicate's funds, the member will suffer deductions for the expenses incurred by the underwriting agency and will have to pay a proportion of the profits to the underwriting agency. The accounts of each of his syndicates are dealt with separately, so that profit commission may be payable in respect of some, even though the member's operations as a whole have resulted in a loss. Further, where an overall profit has been earned it will be subject to reduction by the amount to be paid into the member's personal special reserve fund.

Where a member dies or retires his deposits cannot normally be released until all the underwriting accounts in his name have been run off and closed by way of reinsurance, so that it will be upwards of three years before his Lloyd's affairs are settled. Meanwhile a possible liability hangs over the estate.

Non-underwriting members

In addition to the members of Lloyd's who join for the purpose of underwriting there is a small category of non-underwriting members. This group consists of those who have been underwriting members for many years, but who because of age and the need to re-arrange their financial affairs, cease underwriting but wish to maintain their connection with Lloyd's and their right to use its 'club' facilities.

Annual subscribers

At one time all the members of Lloyd's were called subscribers. Nowadays the class of annual subscriber, as opposed to member, consists mostly of the directors and senior employees of insurance broking concerns. They have the right of entry to the Room. Others who have this right are known as substitutes (in the case of persons employed by underwriters or brokers), or associates (in the case of those whose work requires access to the Room for the benefit of underwriters or brokers, for example, professional persons such as accountants, solicitors, claims adjusters and average adjusters). Associates may also have substitutes. When all these categories are taken into account, there may be as many as 3,000 people in the Room at a busy time.

CHAPTER SIX

LLOYD'S UNDERWRITING AGENTS

The term 'agent' is used in many senses. Anyone who acts on behalf of another is an agent. The insurance world uses the word in various ways to describe particular classes of people. An insurance company will refer to those who receive a commission for introducing business as its agents. Lloyd's Agents, on the other hand, are companies, partnerships or individuals appointed in cities, mostly ports, to provide Lloyd's with intelligence and, when so instructed by underwriters, to carry out surveys and adjust claims; they are not involved in underwriting.

In insurance company practice, underwriting agents are firms appointed to accept insurances on a company's behalf in a place where the company does not have its own underwriter. At Lloyd's an underwriting agent performs quite different functions.

A Lloyd's underwriting agency is a company or partnership (but usually a company) which acts as an agent for an underwriting member at Lloyd's. An underwriting agency has two distinct and separable functions. It may perform either or both. The first is to act for the member in all respects except for managing an underwriting syndicate. This is the role of the Members' Agent. The second function is to manage the affairs of one or more underwriting syndicates. This is the function of the Managing Agent. Of the 303 underwriting agents in September 1982, 105 were Members' Agents only and 35 Managing Agents only. The majority (163) combined both functions. Although the functions are more often than not combined, the work of each category is better understood if considered separately.

Members' Agents

Anyone who contemplates becoming an underwriting member of

Lloyd's needs the services of a Members' Agent, first to guide him through the election procedure, second, to advise him on what syndicates to join, and, third, to oversee the conduct of the business written on his behalf, with special reference to monitoring the syndicates, keeping the member's accounts, collecting the sums due to him, and advising on investment, the creation of personal reserves and taxation.

Lloyd's takes the view that members should be recruited by the traditional method of personal recommendation by existing members, but that a prospective member needs advice, not just from a member, who may not know all about Lloyd's and current aspects of membership, but from a Members' Agent who will do a professional job of furnishing the requisite information. This must include a description of Lloyd's operations and structure, the procedure for becoming a member, the amounts of money involved, the fact that membership is non-transferable, the procedure for joining syndicates and for resigning and the fact that liability is unlimited. Particulars of the business carried on at Lloyd's must be given: for example, the fact that there are four main markets, the number of syndicates and people involved and the procedure for regulation, including the audit. The general principles of taxation need to be indicated and Lloyd's three-year accounting system explained. Attention also has to be drawn to the currency exchange risk if the exchange rate changes between the date of profit computation and distribution. The constitution of the agency and its business must be described and particulars given of the business and results of syndicates the member may be expected to join. The method of calculating and charging syndicate expenses to the member needs to be set out. The proposed form of agency agreement must be produced and explained.

The agency agreement sets out what the agent is authorised to do on the member's behalf and the basis of the agent's remuneration, customarily a fixed fee and a commission on profits. The agreement is usually for a term of three years as no underwriting profits will emerge until then. Thereafter it runs from year to year, subject to six months notice. There is also provision for what happens if the member dies or resigns. Disputes are made subject to arbitration. If the agent gives any remuneration to a person who introduced the member to him, this must be disclosed.

The choice of an agent is probably the most important financial decision an intending underwriting member will have to make in his dealings with Lloyd's. It is difficult for him to shop around, but at least he is entitled to expect that the fullest information shall be made available to him. The Fisher Report (*see* Chapter 9) recommended in 1980 that all agents should be required to furnish Lloyd's Membership Department with details of the terms and conditions they offer and that the

Department should compile a register open to consultation by any applicant for membership or any member contemplating a change of agent.

Before the applicant appears in front of the Rota Committee he or she will have been carefully briefed by the agent. It is vital that the applicant should understand that membership is not an investment like holding shares in a limited liability company, but that if things should go wrong the applicant could be faced with an unlimited liability to fulfil commitments undertaken on his or her behalf.

The agency agreement provides that all premiums required on behalf of a member shall be paid into the Lloyd's Premiums Trust Fund. The agent is empowered to appoint trustees for the fund, but in practice if he is solely a Members' Agent he delegates this power to a Managing Agent. The Members' Agent is responsible for maintaining the member's reserve funds, but the choice of investment for these is usually left to the member, within the classes of investment permitted. The agreement gives the agent a discretion as to how much shall be paid into reserve funds on the member's behalf. The member has the right to examine the agent's books at any time.

The agent is authorised to comply with statutory provisions at home and abroad, and with Lloyd's requirements, to accede on behalf of the member to various agreements at Lloyd's, to collect premiums and other income, and to pay out claims and expenses.

The Members' Agent may or may not be a Managing Agent for some or all of the underwriting syndicates that the member is going to join. If the member is going to join some syndicate for which the Members' Agent is not a Managing Agent, the Members' Agent enters into a sub-agency agreement with the Managing Agent of the syndicate concerned. This agreement will leave the conduct and management of the underwriting to the sole discretion of the sub-agent, who will charge a fixed salary and profit commission as well as a proportion of the agreed management expenses of the syndicate. The Members' Agent retains responsibility for arranging the audit of the accounts of his underwriting members, based on information provided by the sub-agent. A Managing Agent who writes business for his own Names and for Names provided under a sub-agency agreement is said to be writing for a group.

Where underwriting members conduct their underwriting through more than one agent they are required to appoint a co-ordinating agent. It is he who assumes the responsibility for briefing and advising his principal on all aspects of membership and for keeping the Committee informed as to how the underwriting members' premium limit is allocated.

It is the continuing responsibility of every Members' Agent to comply with Lloyd's requirements in respect of his Names and to keep under review the underwriting arrangements so as to ensure that each Name has a proper spread of risk and has reasonable prospects of making a profit. He must therefore monitor the underwriting syndicates concerned and keep the Name informed of progress.

Managing Agents

Managing Agents manage the administration of one or more syndicates employing an active underwriter and an underwriting team for the purpose of transacting insurance. The active underwriter manages the underwriting box and makes the underwriting decisions. The Managing Agent is responsible to each underwriting member of each syndicate concerned. He must make clear to his Names on joining what are the main classes of business written by the syndicate. If a material change in underwriting policy is made subsequently he needs to consider whether the Names ought to be informed. Certainly if there is a change in the active underwriter or in the management or control of the agency the Names must be told.

One example of a change that must be agreed to by the Names concerned is a proposal by a syndicate to write what is called incidental business. A non-marine syndicate, for example, is allowed to write marine insurance, and an aviation syndicate can write marine and non-marine insurance, up to a total of 5 per cent of its premium income. If it has not hitherto been the policy of, say, a non-marine syndicate to write incidental marine business, the agreement of the Names that it should in future be written must be obtained.

Underwriting agencies have assumed increasing importance at Lloyd's in the course of the twentieth-century. Before that, syndicates were small and underwriters themselves found people with capital who were willing to share in their underwriting. Usually these were relations or people known to them in the course of business. In 1865 a broker made a note of the seventy-four underwriters with whom he did business. Fourteen wrote for themselves alone, twenty-eight for themselves and one other, and thirty-two for groups of three, four or six persons. Even by 1900 syndicates were of no more than ten persons as a rule. The Lloyd's Acts of 1871, 1911 and 1925 make no mention of underwriting agencies. It was only in the 1930s that Managing Agencies came to be constituted in the form of limited liability companies. Five of the first six were formed by companies that also transacted insurance broking. In 1954 the Committee of Lloyd's was concerned that if the insurance broking business should be sold the underwriting agency's activities would pass out of the control of Lloyd's. It therefore proposed that the agencies should be separate companies, but this was not achieved until the 1960s. Up to then there were still twenty-five companies acting as broker-agents.

In 1970 By-law 87 was passed to provide for the approval and registration of Lloyd's underwriting agents by the Committee of Lloyd's. The Committee requires that an agency company must have a minimum capital of £10,000. All directors and shareholders must be approved by the Committee. Unless the Committee otherwise allows, only members of Lloyd's may be directors and 75 per cent of the voting shares must be held beneficially by and in the name of members of Lloyd's.

The Fisher Report (see Chapter 9) devoted three chapters to underwriting agents. It received a number of letters of complaint from non-working Names about the underwriting agents' conduct of business and concluded that although there were no means of knowing whether dissatisfaction was widespread, it was at least clear that some Names or intended Names did not receive the standard of service and assistance which they were entitled to expect. Complaints centred on the information available to prospective Names and other information supplied to Names, particularly about the progress of open years. The Fisher Report made a number of recommendations designed to improve the situation. Some of these have already been put into effect. For example, all approved underwriting agents are now required to maintain errors and omissions insurance, that is, insurance against negligence, the dishonesty of directors, partners and employees, and infidelity, with a minimum limit of £500,000. Other recommendations are the subject of active consideration by working parties. Among the recommendations were suggestions that agencies should be approved for a limited time after which continuation of approval should be reconsidered; that the new Council of Lloyd's should take power to ensure that only 'fit and proper' persons should have control over, or be directors or employees of, underwriting agencies; and that interest should be payable on sums due to Names from the date when the sums first become payable. Similarly the Fisher Report recommended that clauses in agency agreements whereby the agent is given wide discretions or unilateral power to vary their terms should be forbidden.

Underwriting agencies and brokers

The most important question considered by the Fisher Report was the relationship between underwriting agencies and brokers. Although there were many underwriting agencies at Lloyd's which had no connection with Lloyd's brokers, the great majority of the larger Managing Agencies were owned wholly or partly by Lloyd's brokers. These agencies accounted for half of Lloyd's underwriting capacity. The Fisher Report pointed out the dangers inherent in this situation, arising from possible conflicts of interest.

To the outsider's eye it is curious that underwriting and broking should be mixed as they have been at Lloyd's. The mixture is of long standing. Both John Julius Angerstein at the end of the eighteenth-century and C. E. Heath a century later were prominent as underwriters and brokers. No differentiation was made in the membership of Lloyd's between underwriters and brokers until 1843 and since then many if not most Lloyd's brokers have elected to be underwriting members rather than mere subscribers. Brokers are always on the look-out for under-writing capacity and underwriters requiring more business have on occasion formed firms of insurance brokers. When underwriting agencies first began to assume importance early in the twentieth-century many were conducted by brokers as part of their business. It was not until the 1950s that separate companies were formed within broking groups to act as underwriting agents. There is a strong tradition that even when a Managing Agency has appointed an active underwriter he acts independently in the interest of his Names and resists any undue pressure from the brokers who control the Managing Agency. But the potential conflict of interest has remained and no disinterested person can fail to approve the separation between brokers and Managing Agents that will result five years from Lloyd's Act 1982.

There is no such conflict of interest in the conduct of a Members' Agency. Brokers are well placed to conduct business there as they have contact with the public and can therefore more easily locate potential Names.

A broker has a duty to his clients to place business on the best terms available, so he will seek to reduce the rate of premium payable whenever this is feasible or may press an underwriter to accept a risk that he would prefer to refuse. An underwriter, on the other hand, has a duty to the members of his syndicate to obtain a rate that will maximise the member's profit. If the underwriter is in effect the employee of the broker he could be subjected to pressure to accept business that he considers undesirable or inadequately rated, or to pay claims where he is not legally liable to do so, in furtherance of the broker's interest. The Fisher Report also saw a possibility that brokers would favour their own syndicates in the placing of their business, so that the rest of the market would be starved of it.

The constitutions of underwriting agencies

Underwriting agents were originally individuals. Nowadays they must be partnerships or limited companies. Nearly all are now companies. Lloyd's has been concerned that such companies should not pass into the control of persons such as insurance companies, who are not under-writing members. The Committee has therefore stipulated that the Articles of Association of any such company should provide for the

Committee to approve all directors and shareholders and that the directors should be members of Lloyd's unless the Committee agrees otherwise; further, at least 75 per cent of the voting shares of the company must be held beneficially by members of Lloyd's unless the Committee agrees otherwise. The company is required to undertake to observe these conditions and to submit for approval any proposed alterations in the Articles of Association, the board of directors, and the ownership of shares. It must not conduct any business other than that of an under-writing agency or sub-agency at Lloyd's.

When the Fisher Working Party reported in 1980 it noted that while the Committee of Lloyd's prescribed a minimum capital for underwriting agency companies it did not require companies to maintain a margin of solvency or to submit reports and accounts. Nor were agencies obliged, as were Lloyd's brokers, to have errors and omissions insurance or indemnity insurance, as were Lloyd's brokers. This was an obvious omission as underwriting agents often hold large balances on behalf of Names. The omission is being rectified.

'Lifeboat' underwriting agencies

Difficulties have arisen in recent years when the operations of an under-writing agency have been suspended. Who is to look after the affairs of the underwriting syndicates, in the case of a Managing Agent, or those of the Names, in the case of a Members' Agent? In respect of the syndicate there are claims to be settled, reinsurances to be arranged, and business continues to come in under binding authorities and open policies (*see* the Glossary for an explanation of this term) until it can be terminated. In 1979 the Committee established two 'lifeboat' underwriting agencies to undertake such work. Their duty was to operate independently of the Committee in the best interest of the Names. In the Sasse affair (*see* Chapter 4), an existing underwriting agency agreed to act, but had a rough passage and eventually resigned. It became involved in litigation with some of the Names concerned in the syndicates.

The underwriting agency called on to act in such circumstances faces many difficulties. Not all Names may be willing to give it full powers unless by the constitution of Lloyd's they are obliged to do so. And it does not follow that what seems the best course of action in the interest of some Names will be seen by other Names as the best course for them. Again, the agency may find that what it considers best for the Names is not necessarily best for the Corporation of Lloyd's as a whole. For example, it may wish to contest the validity of claims under policies on some legal ground when the Corporation, for the sake of its reputation, would prefer that the claims be paid. And the Names, having seen the agency of their choice displaced, for whatever reason, are likely to be hurt and hypercritical of the actions of the agency imposed on them. Faced with a threat to their own solvency through no positive action of their own, they will look about for scapegoats.

CHAPTER SEVEN

UNDERWRITING SYNDICATES AND ACTIVE UNDERWRITERS

UNDERWRITING SYNDICATES

The underwriting syndicate is the basis of Lloyd's operations. Historically it is a product of the Bubble Act of 1720, which confined marine underwriting to two corporations and to individuals and therefore inhibited the development of partnerships to write marine insurance. Even when the prohibition was lifted in 1824 Lloyd's continued to operate on the basis of syndicates, whereby two or more people combined to underwrite not as partners, but as persons each taking his own fraction of a given insurance and assuming no liability for the shares accepted by the other members of the syndicate. In Liverpool, on the other hand, partnerships came to be formed and competed with syndicates.

At Lloyd's a new syndicate can be formed at any time with any number of members, from two to thousands. The large syndicate is a growth of this century. When Cuthbert Heath began underwriting in 1882 he wrote for himself and one other and syndicates hardly ever consisted of more than six people. Since then the average size of syndicates has been getting larger and larger. The number of syndicates actually fell between 1949 (287) and 1973 (276), while the membership of Lloyd's nearly trebled. Table 7.1 shows how the proportion of syndicates to members has been steadily falling.

The Committee of Lloyd's has in general adopted a passive attitude towards the formation of new syndicates and has not sought to control their number. Only once, in 1964, did it seek to control market capacity in order to avoid excessive competition and dilution of the premium available to Names, but the attempt was soon abandoned. It is sometimes felt

Table 7.1 Lloyd's Underwriting Members and Syndicates

	Membership	Syndicates	Proportion of Syndicates to Membership (per cent)
1951	2,913	288	9.89
1961	4,937	280	5.67
1971	6,020	258	4.28
1981	19,136	423	2.21

Source–Lloyd's

that Managing Agents put too many Names into some syndicates, as they draw fees from the Names as well as profit commission and so may benefit in the short-term if not in the long. Agents accused of pressing more underwriting capacity on reluctant active underwriters can point to the need in inflationary times for more capacity in sterling terms if a syndicate is to maintain its real volume of business. They could also point out that within five years of the attempted restriction in 1964 the Committee of Lloyd's was desperate for more capacity. Only if the world economy continues to stagnate and underwriting profits deteriorate further would there be any case for restriction. All the same the appearance of very large syndicates causes concern in some quarters. Their underwriters might be tempted to write larger lines than prudence would dictate, and the failure of any one such syndicate could result in heavy claims on the Central Reserve Fund. There is also the consideration that in some markets, aviation, for instance, the market could grow very narrow if only a few syndicates dominated it.

Major markets

Syndicates operate in one of four main markets, marine, aviation, non-marine and motor. There is also the minor life market. The number of syndicates in each market in 1981 is shown in Table 7.2.

Table 7.2 Lloyd's Syndicates by Market 1981

Marine	160
Aviation	52
Non-marine	159
Motor	46
Life	6
	423

Source–Lloyd's

The growth and size of the four main markets is illustrated in Table 7.3.

Table 7.3 Lloyd's Premium Income and Syndicates by Market 1948–1978

	Marine		Aviation	
	Number of Syndicates	Premiums (£million)	Number of Syndicates	Premiums (£million)
1948	160	61.5	–*	6.2
1958	161	108.0	24	17.3
1968	131	236.1	30	52.6
1978	140	764.2	46	160.5
	Non-marine		Motor	
	Number of Syndicates	Premiums (£million)	Number of Syndicates	Premiums (£million)
1948	100	54.4	20	3.9
1958	94	164.3	21	11.8
1968	72	342.3	31	36.5
1978	128	1044.6	40	192.6

*Aviation not separately recorded
Source –Lloyd's

From the earliest days individual underwriters have written insurance on the lives of persons for short periods such as a year. Such insurances have been common to protect creditors during the period that a loan runs. The Lloyd's system is not appropriate for long-term insurance, which may continue throughout life, or for the granting of an annuity payable for long into the future. For short-term life insurance there is a small but thriving market at Lloyd's. Until 1952 only one syndicate specialised in such life insurance. Now there are six. The term for which they may offer insurance has recently been increased from seven years to ten. This, however, leaves untouched the great bulk of long-term life insurance and there have been demands for many years that Lloyd's should find a way of writing that business. The first attempt to meet these demands was made in 1964 with the formation by certain interests at Lloyd's, notably brokers, of Lifeguard Assurance Ltd, which confined its selling to brokers. Within a few years, however, the company found itself in an unsatisfactory financial position. Further capital had to be raised and the company ceased writing new business. Another company, Lloyd's Life Assurance Ltd, was formed in 1971 with a paid up capital of £4 million, subscribed by underwriting members through the medium of their Premiums Trust Fund. One 'A' ordinary share with special powers is held by the Corporation of Lloyd's. A former Chairman of Lloyd's is the company's chairman. It enjoys a semi-official status without being fully integrated into the Lloyd's market. Lloyd's Life uses as agents only full-time professional insurance brokers.

So far as life business written at Lloyd's is concerned, premiums, about £1 million in 1969, showed no growth in real terms for the ensuing ten years and profit only once reached £250,000. In Lloyd's terms, therefore, life insurance has been negligible.

It can be seen from Table 7.3 that the number of marine syndicates fell over the 30-year period. Non-marine premiums overtook marine in 1949, but the number of non-marine syndicates remains smaller than that of marine syndicates. The motor market set the trend for very large syndicates, some with a thousand or more members, but these are now to be found in other markets too. At the same time very small ('baby') syndicates of a handful of members survive in, for example, the marine market. There appears to be no correlation between the size of a syndicate and its profitability.

Each syndicate is distinguished by a surname or initials (known as a 'Pseudonym') and a number. These are stamped on slips with an indication of the proportion of the insurance accepted by the syndicate, thus enabling the Lloyd's Policy Signing Office to check the transaction and append to each policy the numbers of the syndicates concerned.

Motor syndicates have a special regime of their own. They usually operate at Lloyd's under the umbrella of an 'insurance association', with a name such as Red Star or Service Motor Policies, and have offices at which all the functions performed by an insurance company proper are discharged, including the issuing of policies and the handling of claims. These offices communicate directly with non-Lloyd's brokers as well as Lloyd's brokers. The system of passing every transaction through the Room, which prevails for other classes of insurance, would be hopelessly inefficient for a business constituted of a mass of small insurances on private cars or motorcycles.

Although, as has been said, there are four main markets, they are not separated by impenetrable walls. Aviation, for instance, is often written in the marine market and marine underwriters also commonly accept a proportion of 'incidental' non-marine insurance. In the case of goods in transit it may sometimes be regarded as either marine or non-marine business. The transit may be wholly or partly on land. Americans have a category they call 'inland marine' which has included the so-called 'jewellers' block' – a class of insurance that originated at Lloyd's. The jewellers' block covers the stock of a jeweller against loss or damage. The stock will almost always be on land.

Reinsurance

Reinsurance is a feature of Lloyd's business as it is of all insurance business. The underwriter is always concerned with spreading his risk and limiting the amount he may be called upon to pay for claims, to a sum that he can afford to bear. He is in constant fear of accumulation, that is, the chance that a number of claims can arise at one time or from one cause. To some extent the Lloyd's system restricts the need for reinsurance in that each syndicate can limit the share of any insurance it accepts to a line that is within its means, but there is always the chance that in the case of, say, a shipwreck, an underwriter will be faced with claims on cargo from many different shippers and may in addition have accepted a line on the hull, so that he will be faced with multiple claims. Similarly, in the case of insurance against earthquake or fire following earthquake, he may find himself having to meet losses under a number of separate policies effected by numerous property owners in the area. Reinsurance is the means whereby he keeps his syndicate's losses within manageable limits. By paying a premium to a reinsurer he lays off, or cedes, a part of the risk. Such a reinsurance may either be *ad hoc* in respect of a single policy, when it is termed 'facultative', or under an agreement made in advance to cede a specified part of defined classes of insurance, when it is termed 'obligatory'. The reinsurance agreement is in that case known as a 'treaty'.

Types of reinsurance

Reinsurance may be for a specified proportion of the original insurance. The underwriter may, for example, cede one-half the premium, less a deduction for his expenses in writing the business. This is known as 'quota-share' reinsurance. Alternatively, a reinsurance treaty, known as a 'surplus' treaty, may specify that the reinsurer shall take a share in the direct insurances, which varies according to the class of property concerned, though it remains proportional in some defined way. The reinsurer receives a slice of the premium cake and pays a corresponding slice of the claim.

The alternative form of reinsurance is non-proportional. Here, in return for an agreed percentage of the original premium, the reinsurer agrees to meet losses in excess of a given figure (excess-of-loss reinsurance); or he may agree that, if the loss ratio of a specified class of original insurance exceeds a given percentage, he will meet all or part of that excess (stop-loss reinsurance). Whereas in proportional reinsurance the direct insurer and the reinsurer suffer equally from a given loss, in non-proportional reinsurance their fortunes may differ.

Reinsurance is likely to be less profitable than direct insurance to the extent that the direct insurer, in selecting what business to retain, will naturally seek to keep more of the less hazardous categories for himself.

Reinsurers may themselves reinsure a part of the reinsurance business they accept, in order to limit their own risk. The reinsurance of reinsurance is termed a retrocession.

Reinsurance to close, whereby a syndicate in order to close its third year of account, arrives at an estimate of the cost of running off its liabilities in respect of that year, and pays into another year of account the premium necessary to cover the expected liabilities, is referred to in Chapter 7. Reinsurance to close accounts for a high proportion of Lloyd's reported premium income. Mr Robert Kiln, the well known underwriter, writing in 1980, estimated that of Lloyd's reported net premium income of £1,700 million in 1976, about £700 million related to reinsurance to close.

Abuses of reinsurance

Reinsurance now comprises a very large part of Lloyd's business, especially in relation to overseas business. By its means the spreading of risk by breaking it into manageable fractions enables the capacity of the world insurance market to be mobilised. However, on occasion its use has been abused. Indeed, because at one time reinsurance served gambling purposes, it was illegal in Britain between 1745 and 1864. One form of it, so-called tonner policies, has been used to allow direct insurers to protect themselves against multiple total losses of ships insured by marine underwriters. On occasion such policies have been justified, but sometimes they have given direct insurers a payment in excess of their losses. The Fisher Report in 1980 recommended that where such policies did not have a genuine commercial justification they should be banned. The Committee of Lloyd's accepted the recommendation.

Another abuse which existed until the 1950s was the so-called rollover policy, whereby a syndicate effected a reinsurance with its successor syndicate at an excessive premium. This had the effect of transferring a profit that would have been earned in one year to a subsequent year, thus deferring liability for taxation. The Committee of Lloyd's has sought to outlaw such practices. Its audit manual says: 'Excess-of-loss, stop loss or any other reinsurance contract must not be effected if it has the effect of relieving the syndicate of premium income rather than protecting the syndicate against genuine loss or losses.' Incidents in 1982 have led to the suspicion that in some cases this provision has not been observed and that syndicates have been milked of reinsurance premiums for the benefit of reinsurers. It has even been suggested that persons connected with the syndicates paying the premiums have had an undisclosed financial interest in the reinsurers. Enquiries set on foot towards the end of 1982 will show what truth there is in such allegations.

Specialist syndicates

Within the four main markets syndicates may be known as specialists. For example, there may be syndicates to which one goes for livestock, weather, credit, or legal expenses insurance. Similarly what is called contingency insurance is undertaken by specialists. This description covers insurance against relatively remote possibilities, such as loss arising through the unlikely reappearance of a missing beneficiary after an estate has been shared out. Even in motor insurance there are syndicates specialising in some types of business, for example, the insurance of heavy goods vehicles or of motorcycles, or the insurance of substandard risks, such as motorists who have been convicted of serious offences or young people with sports cars. Others may confine themselves to lighter risks. Another form of specialisation is territorial. A syndicate may be formed to deal primarily with North American non-marine business.

Administration

Most syndicates have offices in or very close to the Lloyd's building. They have a minimal staff, as accounting and policy preparation is done by brokers. They usually have a small claims staff of their own, but much of claims investigation is conducted by bodies such as the Salvage Association and the Lloyd's Underwriters' Claims and Recoveries Office (LUCRO). Alternatively, in marine insurance independent average adjusters (and in non-marine insurance independent adjusters or assessors) are employed, so that claims work consists mainly of reading reports and deciding what action is to be taken on them. Where there are numerous syndicates taking on a risk the reports go to each and conferences may be necessary to decide on the action to be taken. Nearly always agreement can be reached in these conferences, but on occasion views differ. It could happen that some syndicates are willing to settle while others are not.

Lloyd's provides a general statistical service, but syndicates keep statistics for their own book of risks. They receive cards daily from the Lloyd's Policy Signing Office about premium and claims items. A medium-sized non-marine syndicate may receive hundreds of cards which have to be sorted and checked. Underwriters must be kept informed of large items or unusual trends and must establish a record of premiums, net of brokerage, returns and reinsurance, as against net claims. This record is required for each year of account. Reinsurances must be monitored to ensure that limits are not exceeded and that claims are notified to reinsurers and recoveries made from them.

It will be recollected that underwriting accounts are kept open for three years. Throughout the period it is necessary to record the provision required for outstanding claims to which must be added provision for claims incurred, but not reported, known by the acronym of IBNR. The latter may be quite substantial, especially in liability insurance where the seriousness of an occurrence is not always appreciated by the insured

The Underwriting Room at Lloyd's in Napoleonic times. The Napoleonic Wars led to a boom in marine insurance.   *photo: courtesy of Lloyd's*

A gambling policy on the life or arrest of Napoleon, issued to a William Dorrington. Wagers on the lives of public figures were rife in the mid-eighteenth century, although the 1774 Gambling Act required that proof of insurable interest be given.
photo: courtesy of Lloyd's

The Underwriting Room in
mid-Victorian times. The
casualty or loss book records
ship sinkings and other
disasters. Even today entries
are made with a quill pen in
copper-plate handwriting.
photo: courtesy of Lloyd's

Walter Farrant was a famous caller at
the Royal Exchange in the 1890s.
The role of the caller originated in
the coffee houses.
photo: courtesy of Lloyd's

Lloyd's Underwriting Room, pictured on the morning after the loss of the *Titanic*. The casualty boards can be seen at the back, behind the loss book.

photo: courtesy of Lloyd's

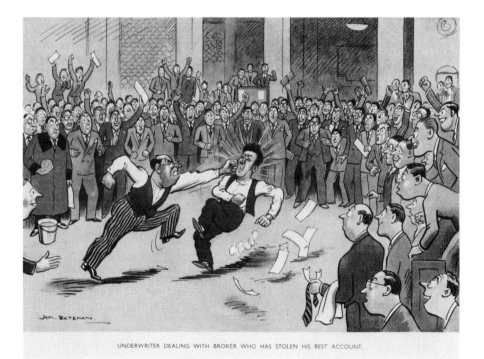

UNDERWRITER DEALING WITH BROKER WHO HAS STOLEN HIS BEST ACCOUNT.

The Underwriting Room at Lloyd's in the 1930s, caricatured by H. M. Bateman.

photo: courtesy of Lloyd's

Lloyd's Underwriting Room in 1949. At the back can be seen the Lutine Bell.
photo: courtesy of Lloyd's

The Underwriting Room in Lime Street. In the centre, new brokers on their first day are being shown the rudiments.
photo: courtesy of Lloyd's

at the outset. When the time comes for closing the earliest of the three years of account it is necessary to decide what provision must be made for claims not already settled. This provision is made by reinsuring the remaining liabilities in the form of 'reinsurance to close', which means that the requisite sum needs to be transferred out of the year of account about to be closed to another account, usually of the same syndicate, but not necessarily so (*see also* Chapter 5). It is essential that reinsurance to close should be adequate. The practice is to apply various tests and to take the value indicated by the highest.

The first test is a minimum percentage prescribed by the Committee of Lloyd's for each sub-class of business. For example, in marine insurances there are sub-classes for 'time all risks' policies, that is, policies giving general cover for a fixed period, for voyage policies (policies covering a specified voyage only) and for war risks policies. For motor there are different minima for direct overseas and direct United Kingdom business.

The second test is the syndicate's evaluation of outstanding liabilities, including provision for the IBNR. Allowance needs to be made for currency fluctuation and inflation. The evaluation is particularly difficult for liability insurance, which is called 'long-tail' business because it may take many years before all the claims relating to a year of account can be quantified. Estimates need to take into consideration the probable amount of damages to which claimants would be entitled if they succeeded in litigation and their chances of claiming successfully either in whole or in part.

Each test is applied separately to sterling, United States dollar and Canadian dollar business.

Even after reinsurance to close has been applied it is necessary to keep statistics showing the year of account to which each claim relates.

Profits and losses

The profitability of underwriting syndicates varies. It is quite possible for a syndicate to make an underwriting loss even in a year when the market as a whole shows a profit for the class of business concerned. The results of most syndicates with a general account will tend to approximate towards the general experience for the class concerned, but selective or specialised syndicates may better the class average. In the years 1948–1978 UK motor insurance showed an underwriting profit of 10 per cent or more in seventeen years of the thirty-one, with smaller profits in twelve other years and a loss only twice, in 1969 and 1970, when the demise of the motor insurance tariff intensified competition from insurance companies. In other non-marine insurance the underwriting profit never reached 10 per cent after 1953 and there were underwriting losses in seven years (1962–1967 and 1974). Marine and aviation insurance descended into unprofitability for four years running in 1964–1967, but otherwise profits were satisfactory in general, exceeding 10 per cent in eighteen years of the thirty-one.

ACTIVE UNDERWRITERS

The fortunes of Names depend on a few hundred men who, as active underwriters, govern the fortunes of the syndicates for which they do business. At one time most underwriters were their own masters and wrote insurances for their own account. Gradually it has become common for them to act on behalf of large syndicates, but still, even though they now have to answer to underwriting agents who control the syndicates, it is their judgement that makes or mars the syndicate's future. Like officers in the services, they are constantly having to make quick decisions which may have momentous consequences for their Names. In the underwriters' case the consequences may not be apparent for years. Their decisions must often be made on the basis of incomplete or imperfect information. When misfortune strikes, as it will from time to time, they must be buoyant and steadfast. Underwriting is no *métier* for the indecisive or the worrier.

The active underwriter may or may not be a member of the syndicate or syndicates for which he writes business. In practice he usually is. He will be remunerated by a fixed fee, normally quite modest, from each member of the syndicate, plus a commission on the trading profits he makes for the syndicate. Successful underwriters command a high remuneration; six-figure incomes are not unknown.

Underwriting skills

The skill of underwriting lies in accepting a book of business that will prove ultimately profitable. This involves knowing the going rates for insurance of particular types and knowing what conditions and exceptions need to be applied to policies. It is only in a few classes of insurance that adequate statistics exist of the historical experience and that one can be sure they are equally applicable to the future.

The statistics of risk

Underwriting depends on the law of large numbers. Suppose that an aircraft valued at £1 million is to be insured against a total loss only and that the chance of such a loss, on the basis of past statistics is one in 100,000. The pure risk cost would therefore be £10 (ignoring the insurer's expenses), but it would be unsafe to insure only a single aircraft at even double that premium because there is always the chance that it would crash and one's capital could be wiped out.

At the other extreme, if one could insure 100,000 such aircraft at £20 (plus a loading to cover expenses) and the past statistics were a valid guide to the future, it is to be expected that only one aircraft would be a total loss and having collected a premium of double the pure risk cost, one could be pretty sure of a large profit after paying for a loss. Of course, there is not such a number of aircraft to insure, but the larger the number that one does insure the greater is the probability that the number of total losses will be only one in 100,000. There is safety in numbers, as it were. The underwriter must therefore be constantly trying to spread his risk over a number of chances and in respect of each chance he must accept only that proportion of the risk that his syndicate can afford to pay. In the insurance of the *Titanic* for £1 million in 1912, for example, the risk was spread over scores of syndicates, each accepting amounts that varied between £75,000 and £500, at a premium of 0.75 per cent. When the *Titanic* sank the loss was therefore spread over hundreds of members of syndicates.

Of course, for some risks an underwriter has no statistics of past experience that are exactly in point. Where, for example, a company which had advertised a reward of £50,000 to go to anyone who found the Loch Ness monster wished to insure against having to pay out, underwriters could not be certain of what the chance might be. They therefore had to make their own judgement of the probability and charge accordingly. Similarly the first underwriters to insure an oil rig or a space shuttle had no statistics directly in point to guide them. Past statistics will not be conclusive as to what happens in the future if some factors change. For example, when jet aircraft were introduced it did not follow that the rate of loss would be the same for them as for turbo-props, and a similar doubt arose when the Concorde started to fly. The underwriter, faced with a novel risk of this kind, will begin by asking for a significantly higher rate than he charges for conventional aircraft and it is likely to take a few years without disaster before the rate settles down to a lower figure.

A statistical basis for rating is not easy to achieve. Statistics depend for their compilation on common units, say, a human life in the case of mortality tables, or a vehicle in the case of road accidents. For fire insurance purposes it is comparatively easy in the case of private dwellings to treat each dwelling as a unit, but factories are not homogeneous. They vary vastly in size and in the hazards attaching to the new processes carried on in them. The Monopolies Commission in its report on the supply of industrial fire insurance in 1972 found that the tariff insurance companies. although they pooled information, had no defensible statistical basis for the rates they charged. For many years they had succeeded in getting rates that yielded overall a good profit, so that competitors such as Lloyd's underwriters, who had a low expense ratio, were able to operate on the basis of cutting the tariff rate by a few per cent.

It can be seen that there are several possibilities in rating. First, a rate can be based squarely on past statistics. Second, it can be adapted by analogy from past statistics for risks that are similar but not identical with those now offered for insurance. Third, it can be based on the rates charged by other insurers. Fourth, it can be simply an informed guess. Lloyd's underwriters make use of all these methods. Of course, wherever competition exists, there will be a difference between what rate they would like to charge and what rate they can actually obtain. In times of severe competition, as at present, rates may be driven down for a time to a point at which premiums are barely adequate to meet losses and expenses. Often the underwriter must depend for his profit on the interest earned on his fund of premiums and reserves before claims have to be paid out. This state of affairs is a potential danger to solvency. Where weather perils and earthquake are concerned, heavy losses occur at irregular intervals and if there is no underwriting profit, even in a good year it is difficult to build up reserves for use in a year when a catastrophe occurs.

Judging risk

The Lloyd's system of individual consideration for each insurance proposed is particularly suitable for large or unusual insurances which merit such treatment. It requires adaptation for run-of-the-mill risks or the mass market for, say, the insurances of individuals. Lloyd's has adopted various devices to deal with these. One such is the open cover whereby the underwriter agrees with a broker to grant insurance on all shipments of a defined category declared by the insured to the broker during the currency of the cover. The insured is given blank certificates detailing the insurance conditions. He completes and returns one of these to the broker whenever a shipment occurs. Another device is the binding authority whereby underwriters give their agents an authority to accept insurances of specified categories on their behalf. The agent is then called a coverholder. It need hardly be said that an underwriter should exercise great caution in 'lending his pen' to anybody. He must as far as possible satisfy himself that the coverholder is experienced and trustworthy and that, in particular, he will not exceed his authority. The troubles of the Sasse syndicate in 1976–1977 were largely attributable to the unsatisfactory use of a binding authority.

In all classes of underwriting two strategies are possible. One is to accept as much business as there is to be had, in the hope that by catering for the vast majority of people one will end up with average risks. This is more or less forced on large companies who cater for the population as a whole. The other is to concentrate on categories or individuals that are considered likely to show exceptionally favourable results. The two strategies of underwriting were illustrated in a law suit a few years ago when an insurance company sought to decline liability under its policy for a theft of the policyholder's property. The company pleaded that the policyholder when applying for insurance had failed to disclose that he had previously been convicted of a criminal offence. If the company had known, it said, it would not have insured him. The question for the court was whether a prudent insurer, if he had known of the conviction, would nevertheless have granted the insurance. A Lloyd's underwriter called as a witness said that he would not insure anyone to whom even a breath of suspicion attached. He would decline to insure anyone who had been accused of a criminal offence even though he had been subsequently acquitted of it. The underwriter of a large insurance company on the other hand said that knowledge of the conviction would not have deterred him from granting insurance.

Lloyd's underwriters have a free choice between the two strategies. Some take one course and some the other. In marine insurance in 1979 the most profitable syndicate was one whose premium income fell slightly, from £21.8 million to £21.4 million, while achieving a considerable balance of premiums over claims; whereas the largest marine syndicate, which was less profitable, showed a rise in income from £39.9 million to £61.25 million. Greater selectivity gave the former a higher rate of profit.

For the insurances of individuals Lloyd's underwriters are competing with large insurance companies who have a network of branches and agents to whom intending insurers can apply. Lloyd's, on the other hand, has a single place of business to which only brokers have access. From the earliest days of motor insurance some Lloyd's syndicates have specialised in the business, from which they have regularly derived more profit than the companies. As mentioned earlier, the method adopted by many syndicates has been either to exercise a more rigorous selection of those they are willing to insure than the companies do, or to identify a section of the market which they think can yield them a profit and to offer favourable terms. A Lloyd's broker has, for example, long offered insurance to categories of policyholders for which most insurance companies are reluctant to cater because of the high risk involved. The substantial rates of premium these syndicates need are not eroded by excessive competition. Thus, one syndicate specialises in motorcycle insurance and others in heavy-goods vehicles. Some offer terms to so-called non-standard or sub-standard risks, such as young drivers with sports cars or drivers who in the past have had their licences suspended for bad driving or for excessive alcohol in the blood.

In the choice of what risks he should insure, and on what terms, an underwriter has a wide discretion, though he may be limited as to the extent to which he accepts insurances outside the market (marine, non-marine, etc.) in which he operates. His choice is also restricted by various market practices and agreements described in Chapter 11. Lloyd's underwriters have hardly ever been parties to the minimum rate (tariff) agreements which have been popular among insurance companies for various classes of fire and accident insurance at home or abroad.

Education and Training

A curious feature of Lloyd's underwriting is that there is no recognised educational qualification. For the great majority experience has been the only school. Many underwriters have risen from the ranks, but there is a strong tendency for family connections to play a part. Cuthbert Heath, exceptional in many ways, was also exceptional in opposing dynasties and refusing to employ more than one member of any family.

The question of education and training for an underwriter remains unanswered. Knowing which business propositions to accept and which to reject is an entrepreneurial skill that cannot be taught as such. Neither Lord Weinstock, managing director of GEC, nor Sir Isaac Wolfson, chairman of Great Universal Stores, both outstandingly successful businessmen, had a specifically business education, though Lord Weinstock, it is true, took a degree in statistics. Entrepreneurial skill is like an ear for music. Either you have it or you do not. But even people with perfect pitch would agree that they benefit from a musical education. At present the only formal course of study in insurance is that for the examinations of the Chartered Insurance Institute. Would-be underwriters should follow this course, but although it has been in existence for over sixty years few appear to have done so. The first Chairman of Lloyd's who was an Associate of the Chartered Insurance Institute was Sir Havelock Hudson (1975). Among others who have qualified is Mr Ian Posgate, referred to in Chapter 4.

While successful underwriting as such cannot be taught, there are many subjects that can help to make an underwriter successful. Statistics, economics and law all come in useful, apart from a knowledge of the technical aspects of insurance and of the working of Lloyd's. All these can be imparted. Formal study should help the would-be underwriter to assimilate the experience he gains from sitting on the box of a senior underwriter. He will then not only see and hear what that underwriter does, but will comprehend more easily the rationale of his decisions. Education, while no substitute for experience, speeds up the process of learning from it. The modern underwriter also feels the need for some education in financial management, with its emphasis on the importance of cash flow, financial risk management and investment.

Recommendations of the Fisher Report

The Fisher Working Party (*see* Chapter 9) pointed out in its report in 1980 that there is some ambiguity in the term 'active underwriter'. The Working Party concluded that it should refer to any individual with authority to underwrite on behalf of a syndicate and who takes the underwriting decisions. This would include persons other than the underwriter named in the syndicate's books, who signs the audit certificate as active underwriter. In practice a deputy underwriter may act and some people act only within a limited authority. The Working Party commented that the Committee of Lloyd's had never sought control over the employment of active underwriters. When registering underwriting agents the Rota Committee might or might not be told whom it was proposed to appoint as an active underwriter. Even where the Rota Committee was informed and took the information into account when deciding to recommend registration, no further control was exercised by the Committee of Lloyd's and the active underwriter might be changed. The Working Party proposed that the Committee of Lloyd's should have a power of veto over the appointment of an active underwriter on the ground that he was not 'a fit and proper person', and that there should be periodical re-registration. There would be a need for appeal machinery for the aggrieved underwriter. It contemplated that the name of a proposed underwriter should be posted in the Room to give an opportunity for objections to be voiced.

The Working Party also drew attention to the desirability of some minimum of experience and qualifications. It recognised that academic qualifications did not guarantee good underwriting. At the same time it believed that Lloyd's should consider introducing a course, with examinations which would in time become obligatory for new underwriters, and that minimum periods of experience should be specified.

Because of the importance of the active underwriter to the welfare of a syndicate the Working Party proposed that the Names should be informed when a new underwriter was appointed and that they should then have the opportunity of withdrawing from the syndicate without the customary three years' notice.

The slip

At the heart of the transaction of insurance in the Room is the slip. This is the document prepared by the broker with particulars of a risk to be insured, for the consideration of underwriters. It will contain particulars of the risk and the material facts about it that the underwriter needs to know, in a largely stereotyped form with many recognised abbreviations. It will be assumed that the insurance is to be in the usual form of Lloyd's policy, unless any proposed departures from it are noted.

The slip is in effect the contract of insurance, but because of the desire of the Inland Revenue in past years to make sure that all marine insurance contracts were expressed in a stamped policy, the Marine Insurance Act 1906 (section 22) provided that in general 'a contract of marine insurance is inadmissible in evidence unless it is embodied in a marine policy'. In non-marine insurance the slip has always been admissible in evidence. Since 1970 when the special stamp duty on marine policies was abolished it has been possible to transact marine business on the basis of a slip policy, meaning that the slip is treated as if it were a policy and no policy is issued unless required for evidential purposes. A slip policy is used, for example, for some forms of reinsurance and for cargo insurance.

A quotation slip is one inviting underwriters to state the rate at which they are prepared to insure. In other words, the underwriter makes an offer to accept the insurance which he can withdraw without notice, though he usually regards it as remaining open for a reasonable time. In any case the underwriter is not bound by initialling a quotation slip, unless he expressly agrees to be bound, as where he inserts the letters H/C (held covered).

Alternatively, a slip (called an 'original' slip) may be one by which the proposer offers to accept insurance at a rate noted on the slip. In that case an underwriter, by initialling the slip unconditionally and applying the stamp which bears his syndicate's number, thereby completes a binding contract of insurance for that share of it that he indicates on the slip (called a line) and the broker becomes liable to him for the relevant premium.

The underwriter's acceptance may be conditional only, as where he notes on the slip that his acceptance is subject to the exclusion of some class of claim or that he requires the insertion of some clause in the contract not previously specified on the slip. Often something remains to be advised, such as the name of the vessel on which cargo for insurance is to be shipped. Alternatively something further needs to be agreed, such as the rate of premium or geographical limits. In either case the initials t.b.a. ('to be advised' or 'to be agreed') will be inserted. If the underwriter also inserts H/C it is an indication that he accepts liability for a loss occurring meanwhile. Otherwise the presumption is that the insurance will not come into effect until the conditions of his acceptance have been fulfilled.

This can be illustrated from the case of *American Airlines Inc.* v. *Hope* [1974] 2 Lloyd's Rep. 301. A slip for one part of an insurance on aircraft hulls stated: 'War Risks exclusion deleted in respect of Hulls only at AP [additional premium] and Geographical Limits t.b.a. L/U [to be agreed by leading underwriter].' Before the premium and the geographical limits had been agreed the aircraft were destroyed on the ground at Beirut by Israeli forces. The courts held that the risk was not covered in the absence of agreement as to geographical limits. It was fortified in this conclusion by the fact that another section of the cover, where there was also a t.b.a. qualification, had been marked H/C whereas this one was not.

Subject to the exceptions of quotation slips and qualified slips there is abundant evidence to support the proposition that when in the London market an underwriter initials a slip, both the proposer and the underwriter are bound immediately. This is certainly so when the slip is 100 per cent subscribed and almost certainly if the slip is only partially subscribed. It is true that in *Jaglom* v. *Excess Insurance Co. Ltd* [1971] 2 Lloyd's Rep. 171, Donaldson J. expressed the view that each underwriter who agrees to take a line is making and not accepting an offer. He considered that there was a contract only when the slip was fully subscribed. If this were so it would mean that a material fact coming to light after an underwriter had initialled and before the slip was fully subscribed would have to be disclosed to him and he would have the opportunity to withdraw. This is not accepted by the textbook writers nor, it would seem, by other judges. For example, in *Eagle Star Insurance Co. Ltd* v. *Spratt* [1971] 2 Lloyd's Rep. 116, Lord Denning remarked: 'Once a syndicate places its signature on a slip it gives its word that it will honour the agreement in it' [unless some qualification such as W.P. (without prejudice) is inserted]. Lord Denning's view seems preferable. Supposing, for example, that reinsurance is being placed on an overdue vessel and that after a line has been accepted by one underwriter word comes that the ship had been lost. One would expect that underwriter to pay his proportion of the loss and to be entitled to a proportionate premium, even though the slip had not been fully subscribed.

On occasion, when a slip is going the rounds an underwriter, after the leading underwriter, makes his acceptance subject to some condition not imposed by the leading underwriter and subsequent underwriters may follow suit. The correct procedure is for the broker to draw this change to the attention of the underwriters who initialled prior to the qualified acceptance and to obtain their assent to the new terms, but this is not always done, as the change would normally be advantageous to them. If the proposed change has not been notified to any given underwriter, it is possible that he would not be able to take advantage of it, so that one slip would cover insurance on certain terms with some underwriters and on different terms with others. J. Staughton accepted that this could happen in *General Reinsurance Corporation* v. *Forsakringsaktiebolaget Fennia* [1982] 1 Lloyd's Rep. 87, when he said 'Market practice abhors a slip on different terms; it is possible but daft.' He was of the opinion that if some underwriters decline to adopt the terms insisted on by the later underwriters the insured has the option to cancel the whole slip, but that a premium for the time the underwriters had been at risk would be payable if the underwriters demanded it.

Another possibility that arises in practice is that the broker showing a slip may obtain acceptances from underwriters that total more than 100 per cent of the insurance asked. When this happens there is said to be an overplacing and at Lloyd's the broker when closing the transaction must 'short close' it, that is, he reduces each line in proportion to arrive at 100 per cent in all. Where, on the other hand, the broker finds himself short of 100 per cent he is not entitled to increase the proportions accepted by each underwriter. The choice then lies between abandoning the attempt to obtain full insurance and accepting the proportion that has been subscribed, or re-submitting the slip at a higher rate of premium in the hope that 100 per cent cover can be obtained.

Descriptions of slips

There are various descriptions of slips. A standard slip is one in a form designed for data processing. A plain slip is one headed by the broker's name only. A special slip, in contrast, is printed for some common type of insurance and relevant particulars of cover are printed on the slip.

An open slip is an original slip providing for a succession of transactions, such as a series of shipments.

A signing slip is a slip copied from the original slip and presented to the Policy Signing Office in lieu of it, the broker retaining the original slip. Where an original slip has been subscribed by both Lloyd's underwriters and insurance companies, the broker prepares separate signing slips to enable the respective Lloyd's and companies' policies to be prepared. Similarly signing slips are used to record successive items under open slips and reinsurance treaties. These are also called 'off slips'. The initials of the leading underwriter only suffice to authenticate them.

A slip agreement may be needed to confirm proposed alterations to an insurance or special agreements after an insurance has been concluded. This will often require the initials of all the underwriters concerned. If there are six or more a honeycomb slip is used. It is printed with a number of squares for insertion of the numbers of the syndicates involved in their order on the original slip, and facilitates ensuring that all the parties have initialled.

Renewals are dealt with by renewal slips.

CHAPTER EIGHT

LLOYD'S BROKERS

Development of Lloyd's broking

Insurance brokers have always been vital to the Lloyd's market. In the seventeenth and much of the eighteenth-century, when Lloyd's had no formal organisation, the would-be assured had to rely on a broker to find underwriters for his risk, prepare the policy and obtain the signatures to it. The underwriters, for their part, looked to the broker and not to the assured for payment of the premium, and settled claims in their account with the broker. The broker was thus the agent of the assured for the purpose of arranging the insurance and collecting any claims. His position contrasted with that of persons appointed as agents by an insurance company for the purpose of getting business for that company in return for a commission on the premium.

At the outset brokers called themselves office-keepers as they, unlike underwriters, worked from an office. They did not confine their placings to Lloyd's and often had to scour the City to find underwriters. For a long time brokers did not have an exclusive right to place business at Lloyd's, though by 1800 they in fact placed most of it. During the Napoleonic Wars, however, many merchants who were subscribers to Lloyd's and therefore had access to the Room took to placing insurances there. Between 1800 and 1810 merchants placed as many insurances at Lloyd's as did the brokers. Subsequently the advantage of using a broker must have become increasingly apparent and the brokers eventually gained a *de facto* monopoly of placing business at Lloyd's. Curiously, however, they are not even mentioned in the Lloyd's Act 1871.

Firms of brokers became increasingly numerous in the nineteenth-century. A London directory of 1836 lists eighty-nine and includes the names, still found among Lloyd's brokers today, of Robert Bradford, Henry Dumas and Alexander Howden. In 1870 there were 158 firms. Nearly all of these confined themselves to marine insurance. Fire insurance was in its infancy at Lloyd's and the members of the fire insurance companies' association (the Fire Offices' Committee) showed reluctance to pay commission on fire business to brokers unless they applied to a company to become its agent, which many brokers were reluctant to do. The FOC made an exception only for seven or eight specified brokers.

With the development of many classes of non-marine insurance at the end of the century, brokers often led the way in identifying the need for new forms of cover and finding a market, usually at Lloyd's, where underwriters were prepared to innovate. Insurance against burglary and 'all risks', loss of profits insurance and credit insurance are examples. Brokers helped to form early syndicates for motor and aviation insurance.

Until after World War I there was no formal separation between underwriting and broking. Both Angerstein and Cuthbert Heath formed broking businesses while being prominent underwriters. Henry Poland, while working for an underwriter, formed a broking partnership in 1883 and retained this business when he became an active underwriter for a small syndicate in 1885. Harry Wrightson was an underwriting member when he formed Matthews, Wrightson & Co. in 1901. Two years later his firm acquired an active underwriter and formed the first purely non-marine syndicate at Lloyd's for which it acted as underwriting agent. It seems that underwriters such as Poland formed broking firms partly for the purpose of placing their own reinsurances.

Brokers competed freely among themselves. In 1906 some of them, including the Lloyd's brokers Walter Faber and David Willis, formed an Association of Insurance Brokers and Agents, later to be the Corporation of Insurance Brokers. One of the Association's objects was 'to check the promiscuous appointment of agents by insurance companies'. In 1910 Lloyd's Insurance Brokers' Association was established as a counterpart to the Lloyd's associations of underwriters.

Many firms of insurance brokers combined ship-owning, ship chartering and even general trading with the broking business. Bowring's is the most notable example. Brokers have also founded or acquired insurance companies.

Developments in the twentieth-century

The twentieth-century has seen the rise of insurance broking, as more risks became insurable and businesses in particular felt the need for advice in the diagnosing of their insurance needs and the placing of their business. At the beginning of the century few brokers had more than one place of business or employed more than a score of people. Lloyd's brokers however were already beginning to think internationally. C. E. Heath & Co. had a large American connection and was soon to be rivalled by C. T. Bowring. The great period of growth came after World War II when all the leading Lloyd's brokers extended their operations territorially. At home they either opened up branch offices or, more commonly, acquired the businesses of provincial brokers. Abroad they developed joint ventures with local brokers or entered markets themselves.

Broking has proved highly profitable for efficient organisations. The value of big broking concerns grew inconveniently large from the taxation point of view where the shares were held by a few individuals only, and brokers had to consider turning themselves into public companies. The first to do so were C. E. Heath & Co. Ltd. in 1962. A number of others followed suit in the next fifteen years, culminating with Willis, Faber & Dumas Ltd, which, with an issued capital of £11.4 million in 1976, half of it held by nine directors, had made a profit of £10 million in 1975. The company then employed 2,600 people in the United Kingdom and 1,000 overseas.

A public company is vulnerable to take-over by outsiders in a way that a private company or partnership is not. In 1972 C. E. Heath & Co. Ltd found that the Excess Insurance Co. Ltd which had been founded by Cuthbert Heath and which still had directorial links with C. E. Heath and Co. Ltd was contemplating a take-over bid without the knowledge of the Heath directors. The Chairman of Lloyd's, when informed, took the view that Lloyd's would not approve the ownership of a Lloyd's broker by an insurance company. He regarded the Lloyd's and company markets as separate and distinct and feared the prospect that insurance companies, by gaining control of Lloyd's brokers, could eventually dominate the Lloyd's market. In face of the opposition from Lloyd's the merger plan was abandoned. However, a tendency towards forming bigger broking units continued to be felt. Many medium-sized Lloyd's brokers were absorbed. The needs of multinational trading companies for insurance services on their world-wide business called for brokers who could advise and act on an international basis.

Large American insurance brokers already had close ties with particular Lloyd's brokers. Some decided that the acquisition of Lloyd's brokers was the best course. The Committee of Lloyd's had adopted a rule that shareholdings in a Lloyd's broker by non-Lloyd's insurance interests should generally be limited to 20 per cent of the share capital. Some intended acquisitions of shares by American brokers were thwarted by this rule, but the pressure to acquire a stake in existing Lloyd's brokers continued. In 1980, with the acquiescence of the Committee of Lloyd's, the American brokers Marsh & McLennan acquired the Bowring Group which included one of the largest Lloyd's brokers, subject to an undertaking that the latter would be left under the control of its directors who would have complete authority to carry out any requirements of the Committee of Lloyd's. Another American broker, Alexander & Alexander, sought to reach a joint working arrangement with Sedgwick Forbes, a very large Lloyd's broker, but it was not possible to find a satisfactory basis and Alexander & Alexander thereupon acquired Alexander Howden, a group with a company in the first division of Lloyd's brokers. In both the acquisitions mentioned, the issue to shareholders of shares in the American companies was involved and those companies acquired a Stock Exchange quotation for their own shares. Some idea of the value of large broker companies can be obtained from Table 8.1 which shows the Stock Exchange valuation of their ordinary shares on 24 September 1982.

Table 8.1 Capitalisation Value of Insurance Broking Groups as at 24 September 1982

United States brokers	£ million
Marsh & McLennan	814.1
Alexander & Alexander	365.7
United Kingdom brokers	
Sedgwick	412.5
Willis Faber & Dumas	196.5
C. E. Heath	104.9
Minet Holdings	103.8
Stewart Wrightson	43.0
Stenhouse	38.7
Hogg Robinson	34.7

Source – The Times (28 September 1982)

Marsh & McLennan's capitalisation exceeded that of all United Kingdom insurance companies except the Prudential.

The large insurance broking group of today is likely to comprise a main Lloyd's broking company, one or more Lloyd's underwriting agency companies, a non-Lloyd's underwriting agency company, an insurance company, and separate broking subsidiaries for specialist classes (such as reinsurance, credit or life and pensions insurance, or insurance for regions in the United Kingdom). In addition it will have consultant companies, such as benefit or risk management companies. It may also own companies for non-insurance activities, such as shipping, ship-broking, travel agencies or leasing.

The work of insurance brokers

In the simplest case someone who wants an insurance instructs an insurance broker to place it on his behalf. The insurance broker becomes his agent for that purpose. With the broker's knowledge of the market he approaches suitable insurers. In the case of insurances at Lloyd's, the broker prepares a slip, seeks competitive quotations from underwriters and obtains subscriptions to the slip. Once the slip is 100 per cent subscribed he closes the transaction through the Lloyd's Policy Signing Bureau. The account between the broker and the underwriters is kept in the central accounting system. The broker is debited with the premium and credited with any claims he may have to pay subsequently on the insurer's behalf. The broker is remunerated by a commission on the premium and a discount on the claim.

Alternatively, a client may in the first place simply ask the broker to report on his insurance arrangements generally and make recommendations which he may or may not adopt. The broker seeks to improve on his client's existing programme. For example, he may identify risks which should be insured and are not, or risks which are insured, but are not worth insuring. Often the broker will find that existing policy wordings need to be widened in his client's interest or that the sums insured on property are inadequate or the limits of liabilities covered are too low. The broker may find it possible to get reductions in the rates of premium charged. If there is a good prospect that the client will entrust his insurance programme to the broker there is likely to be no charge for the report. Alternatively, such a report may be prepared in return for an agreed fee, where the client does not contemplate changing from his existing broker, but simply wants a second opinion.

Brokers often find it necessary to employ specialists, such as fire or security surveyors. They may recommend the client to use the services of risk management or security consultants or professional surveyors or valuers.

Brokers and reinsurance

Lloyd's brokers, or their reinsurance broking subsidiaries, play an important role in international reinsurance. Lloyd's underwriters were pioneers in the development of excess-of-loss reinsurances and access to them is available only through a Lloyd's broker. In addition underwriters themselves employ brokers to place their own reinsurances.

The growth of international reinsurance in the twentieth-century has led to Lloyd's brokers travelling the world in search of reinsurance business. Many reinsurance arrangements involve numerous underwriters and insurance companies who not only accept reinsurances, but also retrocede parts of these to yet other insurers throughout the world.

Brokers may be given facilities for accepting reinsurances on behalf of groups of insurers. A commission is payable to them both on the original reinsurances and on any subsequent retrocessions they may be instructed to arrange. Although rates of commission may be low, large volumes of premium can be concerned.

Regulation of Lloyd's brokers

Until the coming into force of the registration requirements of the Insurance Brokers (Registration) Act 1977 anyone was at liberty to style himself an insurance broker, though not, of course, a Lloyd's broker. The status of being a Lloyd's broker arose by a side-wind from Lloyd's Act 1871 which stated Lloyd's Fundamental Rule 5: 'A member shall not open an insurance account in the name of any person not being a member or subscriber.' Further, by-law 25 made under the Act provided that any firm or company with a partner or director who is a member or annual subscriber of Lloyd's may, if permitted by the Committee of Lloyd's, show a brokerage account in the Room on payment of a subscription.

Thus it has come about that the status of a Lloyd's broker with the right to conduct business in the Room is confined to brokers approved by the Committee of Lloyd's. The Committee imposes various conditions. Applicant brokers must have a paid up capital of at least £50,000 and a solvency margin varying from £25,000 to £1 million according to the amount of business transacted. They must demonstrate their knowledge of the working of the Lloyd's market and their ability to carry out the necessary administrative tasks such as policy preparation. Since 1974 all new directors of Lloyd's brokers have been required to become annual subscribers to Lloyd's if they are not already members.

Like all brokers Lloyd's brokers must be registered with the Insurance Brokers' Registration Council and must comply with that body's rules and code of conduct. Where the rules overlap with those of Lloyd's, the Lloyd's requirements are in general more stringent: Lloyd's brokers are subject to discipline by both the Council and by Lloyd's. There could in theory be a conflict of jurisdiction, but it is not thought that any difficulty will in practice arise. Some Lloyd's brokers were among the greatest enthusiasts for the registration of brokers instituted by the 1977 Act. As an earnest of their solidarity with non-Lloyd's brokers, upon the formation of the British Insurance Brokers' Association in 1977, Lloyd's brokers disbanded the Lloyd's Insurance Brokers' Association, transferring its staff and functions to a newly constituted Lloyd's Insurance Brokers' Committee which operates as an autonomous section within the BIBA and is also answerable to the Committee of Lloyd's.

In Lloyd's practice the broker assumes the responsibility of acting for his client in the presentation of any claim against underwriters. In all his work he must exercise professional care and skill. He is subject to the code of conduct of the IBRC which requires him *inter alia* to place the interests of his client above all other considerations.

The broker is always in the first place the agent of the insured. He therefore needs a mandate; an authority to act. This may be oral or by implication or in writing. The insurer who deals with a broker is entitled to assume that the broker has such a mandate unless he has good reason to believe the contrary. If the broker acts without authority and the insurer sustains loss as a consequence the insurer can sue him for breach of warranty of authority.

There are many circumstances in which a broker may find himself liable to his client if the broker has been guilty of some error or omission in the course of his work. It has been mentioned that the insured is under a legal duty to disclose to a potential insurer all facts about the risk proposed for insurance that a prudent insurer would wish to know, namely, all material facts. If a broker, knowing of some material fact, has failed to disclose it, the insurer will be entitled to decline liability for a claim under the policy. In that case the insured will be able to sue the broker for the loss he has sustained. Similarly, if a broker failed to effect an insurance that he was instructed to effect, and a loss that should have been insured proves not to have been covered, the broker will be liable. In one recent case an insured who had for many years used the services of broker 'A' suddenly withdrew the broker's mandate and went to broker 'B' who wished to discontinue existing insurances and place them with other insurers. Broker 'A', believing that a new insurance had been effected, instructed the existing insurers to cancel their policy and they did so. A loss then occurred and it was found that a new insurance had not been effected. Broker 'A' was held liable for the loss. It is mandatory on brokers to hold a professional indemnity insurance with a high limit of indemnity.

Brokers are in effect the marketing arm of Lloyd's. Often they take the initiative in devising new forms of policy. From their experience of the needs of particular trades they may draft policy wordings and conditions that give the wide cover desirable for policyholders which may go beyond the customary cover, and they may seek out insurers who will give the extended cover by using the brokers' clauses.

In Lloyd's practice the broker, when he places an insurance with the underwriter, accepts a liability to the underwriter for the premium. Using legal fictions the courts say that broker and underwriter deal with each other as principals and that the underwriter is deemed to have advanced the premium to the broker on credit, the broker then becoming responsible for paying it back to him in due course. The underwriter cannot sue the insured for the premium, but the insured, if he chooses, may recover directly from the underwriter any return of premium that becomes payable even where the insured has not paid his premium to the broker. The broker has a lien on the policy for payment of the premium.

As mentioned above, brokers receive credit from underwriters for premiums, so large sums are often in their hands for a period of months. They are obliged by Lloyd's to place premiums in a special account segregated from their own moneys and thus safe from creditors if they should become insolvent. They derive a significant part of their income from the interest on these accounts and, unlike solicitors, they are not obliged to credit their clients with this interest.

At Lloyd's it is the custom for claims to be made against underwriters on the insured's behalf by a Lloyd's broker. In straightforward claims the broker endorses the amount of the claim on the policy, prefixes the word 'settled' and on obtaining the underwriters' initialled agreement, debits their account with the amount and settles in account with the insured, deducting a collecting commission of 1 per cent. An exception to settlement in the normal monthly account can be made where the claim is for a total loss or for a large sum, in which cases the underwriters pay the claim separately, as a rule within seven days. This is termed a special settlement.

Where a claim requires investigation or where underwriters dispute it, it used to be the case that underwriters would ask the broker to obtain a report from adjusters or solicitors on their behalf and to circulate among the underwriters these reports and the comments of the leading underwriter or claims adviser. This meant that the broker was in the position of acting simultaneously as an agent of two parties – the insured and the underwriters – with potentially conflicting interests. In two cases a few years ago, where brokers had obtained reports and circulated them to underwriters, the insured claimed the right to see the reports. The brokers refused saying that they were acting in accordance with the usage of Lloyd's. The judges considered that any such usage was unreasonable and could not be enforced; a person should not act as the agent of two parties at the same time unless he has obtained the informed consent of both principals.

Lloyd's way of doing business was evolved in marine insurance and is not suitable for, say, motor insurance, where potential clients are widely dispersed and often find themselves in need of immediate cover. Much motor insurance is placed through local brokers who are not Lloyd's brokers and it was found expensive and time-wasting to require that all correspondence should pass through Lloyd's brokers. Large underwriting syndicates were therefore formed and in the 1960s given permission to deal direct with non-Lloyd's brokers on condition that such a broker should be sponsored by a Lloyd's broker who would accept liability to the underwriters for the premium in return for a small overriding commission.

Lloyd's brokers are restricted by Lloyd's regulations as to advertising. Printed advertisements for a Lloyd's broker must in general be limited to the broker's name, telephone number and a brief description of the organisation and services offered. However, where a special insurance scheme is advertised, the details may be expanded to refer to the terms and conditions of the insurance cover available. Lloyd's motor syndicates may advertise individually or in conjunction with outside agents provided they simply identify themselves as motor insurers at Lloyd's. Any proposal going beyond that must be submitted for approval.

Commission

Insurance brokers are commonly remunerated by a commission which is paid by underwriters. In marine insurance premiums are subject to a deduction of 5 per cent brokerage and 10 per cent discount. The discount used to be calculated on the premium after deduction of brokerage, so that it was only 9.5 per cent. Nowadays a flat 15 per cent is deducted, but brokers continue to pass on the discount at 9.5 per cent only, so that their commission on marine insurance is effectively 5.5 per cent. This is subject to a number of exceptions. In particular, brokerage on cargo insurance is 7.5 per cent. The discount, which was originally one for cash, is reduced to 7.6 per cent where, as often in hull insurance, the premium is paid by instalments; and on occasion brokers keep the 10 per cent discount for themselves. For other classes of insurance commission rates vary between 10 per cent and 20 per cent or more.

An agent such as a broker is in law required to disclose to his client any remuneration he receives from a third party. The law assumes that it is within the knowledge of clients that the broker derives his remuneration from commission payable by insurers. By a regulation of the Insurance Brokers' Registration Council an individual client must be told the amount if he asks. If the broker receives commission for recommending his client any outside services or products, such as a sprinkler system, he must tell the client of this.

It is often argued that as a broker acts for the insured he ought to receive his remuneration from the insured and not from insurers. Critics say it is unsatisfactory that the higher the amount insurers charge the more commission the broker receives, and that it would be more equitable if the insured were to pay a fee related to the work done by the broker. However that may be, remuneration by commission is the method adopted throughout the world for insurance brokers' remuneration, though in the United Kingdom a fee basis is used in some circumstances. Fees may, for example, be charged where brokers advise the insured on how to manage his risks, provide an inspection service or report on a company's insurances without the prospect of themselves placing the business.

Insurance brokers and underwriting

As mentioned before, a question about Lloyd's that has long concerned outside critics is the extent to which it is legitimate for persons to act both as brokers and underwriters in insurance transactions. The two functions have always been intertwined at Lloyd's, but there are obvious possibilities for conflicts of interest.

The Insurance Companies Act 1974, section 64, started to tackle the problem by providing that regulations could be made for requiring any person connected with an insurer to reveal his connection when inviting anybody to effect an insurance with the insurer concerned. The Insurance Companies (Intermediaries) Regulations 1976 were the result. They apply both to insurance companies and to Lloyd's syndicates. In the case of Lloyd's brokers the disclosure requirement can be satisfied by using the expression 'Lloyd's broker' when issuing the invitation to insure at Lloyd's, without referring specifically to the names of the underwriters concerned. (Some of the directors of the Lloyd's broking company concerned are likely to be underwriting members of Lloyd's and may be members of syndicates with which the business is eventually placed.) In the case of brokers who have a relationship with an insurance company the relationship must be clearly stated.

As mentioned in Chapter 6, the Fisher Working Party concluded that a break needed to be made between Lloyd's brokers and Lloyd's Managing Agencies. The report recommended that brokers should, within a reasonable time, be obliged to divest themselves of the ownership or control of Managing Agencies, though no objection was seen to their continuing to own or control Members' Agencies. The Committee of Lloyd's, in the draft Bill it submitted to Parliament, left the question to be decided by the proposed new Council of Lloyd's. The Commons committee which considered the Bill concluded that divestment should be mandatory and must therefore be expressly provided for. Indeed, the committee went further and proposed that Managing Agents and Members' Agents should be divorced from each other, that is, completely separated. The Committee of Lloyd's submitted these two questions, divestment and divorce, to a vote by the membership. The vote went in favour of divestment, but against divorce. The Commons then gave way on divorce, and a clause requiring divestment was inserted in the Bill. Some leading brokers continued their opposition to the clause, but did not succeed in their campaign against it. By sections 10 to 12 of Lloyd's Act 1982 a Lloyd's broker may not be a Managing Agent and a Managing Agent may not be a Lloyd's broker, but a five year period is allowed for divestment by persons who before the Act fulfilled both functions. (*See* Chapter 9 for further details of the Fisher Working Party and the Lloyd's Act 1982.) No separation of brokers and Members'

Agents is, however, required. Members and employees of Lloyd's brokers can continue to be Names and so passively involved in under-writing. And Lloyd's brokers are not debarred from owning and running Managing Agencies for underwriting by the insurance companies they represent, though they must of course disclose their interest in these companies in accordance with the Insurance Companies (Intermediaries) Regulations 1976.

CHAPTER NINE

THE GOVERNMENT OF LLOYD'S

The government of Lloyd's is in transition. It will be necessary to begin by describing how it operated in 1982 and then to consider how far the position is modified by the new Lloyd's Act, passed in July 1982.

The Government of Lloyd's up to 1982

The Society of Lloyd's was first incorporated by Lloyd's Act 1871, to which modifications were made by further Acts of 1888, 1911, 1925 and 1951. By-laws were made under the Acts.

In 1981 the Committee of Lloyd's, which administered the affairs of the Society, consisted of sixteen members, four of whom retired each year. Any retiring member, unless he was Chairman at the time of his retirement, was not eligible for re-election for a year. Members were elected to the Committee by all members of Lloyd's present at a general meeting held in November each year. The Committee elected one of its members to be Chairman and two to be Deputy Chairmen, one senior and one junior. The Committee met weekly.

The chairmanship most commonly went to a senior active underwriter, though occasionally a broker was elected. The Chairman was usually re-elected for at least one year and sometimes for more. At one time it was expected that a past Chairman would not return to active underwriting, but there have been exceptions. Election as Deputy Chairman was not necessarily a stepping-stone to the chairmanship.

To be Chairman of the Committee had become an increasingly onerous task. Lloyd's Act 1871 provided for him to be remunerated, but in practice he acted without remuneration. His duties were both business and social. Like the Lord Mayor he commonly made at least one overseas trip during his year of office. In addition to presiding over the Committee he was the public face of Lloyd's and so was often called on to make public pronouncements or to state the Lloyd's view on some difficult question. He and his deputies often had to tackle difficult situations, to mediate in disputes or to force or persuade reluctant parties to take a proper course of action. A Chairman was likely to have a pretty good view of what his Committee's reaction would be in a particular situation, but in facing hostile bowling he was not always as quick on his feet as a politician. He might sometimes block a ball which should have been hit for six, or vice versa. A capacity to eat one's words gracefully was sometimes called for.

When Lloyd's Act 1871 was passed the chairmanship was held by a banker-politician who seldom attended the Committee. The Fisher Working Party considered in 1980 whether a professional Chairman was called for nowadays, but came down strongly against the idea: 'We do not believe that a Chairman could carry out his role or exercise authority without long experience of working at Lloyd's and without being personally known to many working members at Lloyd's.' The Working Party did however consider that the Chairman should be relieved as far as possible from involvement in the day-to-day decision-making process. It is difficult to see how this can be achieved so long as the Committee meets weekly.

By-laws required the approval of a general meeting, confirmation by a subsequent general meeting held within twenty-eight days, and approval by the Recorder of the City of London.

The power to exclude anyone from membership also rested with a general meeting. An 80 per cent majority was required. The Committee had the power to suspend membership for up to two years if a member had committed a discreditable act or default, but he was entitled to appeal to a general meeting.

General meetings were held twice a year, but might be called more frequently.

The responsibilities of the Committee could be grouped under five heads. First, the Committee had the power to specify the terms of membership and to admit members. Second, it admitted underwriting agents and Lloyd's brokers and regulated them. Third, it provided rooms and other services for underwriting. Fourth, it assumed responsibility for checking the security behind Lloyd's policies and for providing the returns required by the government in respect of Lloyd's business. Fifth, it was responsible for safeguarding the interests of members, the reputation of Lloyd's, and its legal interests throughout the world.

The Committee had the power to appoint committees and sub-committees including persons who were not members of Lloyd's. An important committee was the Rota Committee, which interviewed applicants for membership of Lloyd's, accompanied by their under-writing agent. The Rota Committee checked that each applicant's papers made him or her eligible and that the applicant appreciated the unlimited liability being undertaken and the extent of the freedom granted to the underwriting agent, which could make or mar the applicant's fortunes. The Committee of Lloyd's considered the recom-mendation of the Rota Committee and voted on it by secret ballot.

The Committee of Lloyd's in 1980, a typical year, consisted of eleven underwriters (five marine, four non-marine, one aviation and one motor), three brokers and two underwriting agents. The descriptions relate to the members' prime interests. Thirteen members were in fact directors of underwriting agencies. Elections to the Committee were regularly contested with anything from 700 to 1,700 members voting. All, or almost all, of those voting would have been Working Names, that is, underwriting members working at Lloyd's.

The Fisher Working Party

By 1978 the creak in the machinery of Lloyd's governance had become audible to the ears of those outside. It clearly needed a thorough over-haul. Names in the Sasse syndicate were claiming that their losses stemmed at least in part from a failure of the Committee of Lloyd's to exercise supervision and enforce its own regulations (*see* Chapter 4). Late in 1978 the Committee appointed a Working Party under the chairmanship of Sir Henry Fisher, a former High Court judge, to enquire into self-regulation at Lloyd's. The other six members were a merchant banker, the director of the Royal Institute of International Affairs, and four Lloyd's men (two underwriters, a broker, and an underwriting agent). The Working Party's report was published on 27 June 1980. It contained seventy-nine recommendations.

The report concluded that Lloyd's needed a new governing body and a Council, which would include, besides the sixteen active members of Lloyd's constituting the Committee, six non-working Names and three non-members of Lloyd's (the latter to be nominated for co-option and approved by the Governor of the Bank of England). The Council would have the power, previously exercised by a general meeting, to make by-laws, subject to the approval of majorities both of the working members of Lloyd's on the Council and of the remaining members on the Council, each of its two constituencies voting separately. The report recommended that the Council should also have the power to suspend or exclude members and that a mechanism of a disciplinary committee and an appeals tribunal should be established. It was contemplated that the Committee of working members would continue to do most of the day-to-day work and that the Council could delegate to it power to make regulations regarding the conduct of insurance business.

The Working Party considered that the proposed Council should undertake an overall responsibility towards Names and should exercise a supervisory role over underwriting agents. Complaints had been received from some Names as to their treatment. There appeared to be in some cases a lack of service provided for them, nor were prospective Names always given enough information at the outset to enable them to decide which syndicates to join. The report recommended that there should be more disclosure by some underwriting agents who did not come up to the best standard. A mandatory form of agreement between the Name and the underwriting agent was needed, though it could be subject to variations, for example, as to the agent's remuneration. Agents should not be permitted to contract out of their legal liability to Names.

The report recommended that the registration of underwriting agents should be periodically reviewed. All underwriting agents should be required to have insurance against errors and omissions. Where a managing agent had to be replaced the Committee should have the power to substitute another. The appointment of an active underwriter should be notified to the Committee, which should have discretion to satisfy itself that the appointee was a fit and proper person and to intervene if at any time it became apparent that the active underwriter was incapable of performing his duties satisfactorily.

The report considered that power was needed for the Council to make by-laws to govern the approval and discipline of Lloyd's brokers. The brokers' status should be reviewed from time to time. The Council should also have power to limit the size of syndicates if necessary to avoid serious prejudice to Lloyd's or Lloyd's policyholders.

Regulation up to the time of the report had often involved a requirement for undertakings to be given by new members, brokers or underwriting agencies which had not always been imposed on those already operating. The Working Party recommended that in future more matters should be covered by by-laws or regulations rather than by undertakings, conditions or requirements imposed on admission. A volume containing all by-laws and regulations should be published and kept up to date.

The most controversial part of the Working Party's report was its proposal that within about five years Lloyd's brokers should be required to divest themselves of an interest in managing agencies and vice versa. This cut across the practice of centuries, during which broking and underwriting had been transacted by closely linked persons. However, its logic was irresistible. The Lloyd's members of the Working Party were themselves sure that the conflict of interest was not only potential, but actual, though they said that serious abuses had so far been rare.

The report pointed clearly to what needed to be done.

Lloyd's Act 1982

The Fisher Report contained in an appendix a draft Bill to give effect to its recommendations. Consultation with members and market associations showed that 71 per cent of members favoured the promotion of a new Act of Parliament. On 4 November 1980 a meeting of members, called the Wharncliffe meeting, was held at the Albert Hall, with 3,722 members present. A resolution in favour of a Bill prepared by the Committee was supported by 13,219 members (out of 18,552). The Bill as presented to Parliament later in the month did not follow exactly the lines of the Fisher draft, but was substantially the same. Some die-hards objected to the separate representation of external members on the proposed Council. Some external members considered their representation inadequate. The six non-working Names out of the twenty-five proposed by Fisher were eventually increased to eight out of twenty-seven. The Fisher Working Party had come out by a majority of six to one in favour of the separation of insurance brokers from managing agencies. The draft Bill merely empowered the new Council if it chose, to effect the separation. Many people did not accept this. There were also objections to the Fisher recommendation that the proposed Council of Lloyd's should be made immune from suit by members of the Lloyd's community for acts or omissions under Lloyd's Act.

The Committee's Bill was submitted to Parliament on 26 November 1980. On 24 March 1981 the House of Commons approved it by 206 votes to 42, but objections by interested parties caused the Bill to be referred to the Opposed Bill Committee which sat for seven days in May 1981.

As mentioned in Chapter 8, the Commons committee eventually declared itself in favour not only of mandatory divestment by insurance brokers of their interest in Managing Agencies and vice versa, but also of divorce, that is, the separation of Managing Agencies from Members' Agencies as well. These proposals were put by the Committee of Lloyd's to the Names who in a ballot approved of divestment, but not of divorce. The Commons committee gave way and the road appeared clear for the Bill. Some opposition remained. First, objection was taken to the extent to which the Bill proposed to exempt the Society of Lloyd's from liability to any member of the Lloyd's community, including members, Lloyd's brokers, underwriting agents and past or intending members. This problem was solved by amendments which made it clear that the Society remained liable for libel or slander or for the acts of employees carried out in a routine or clerical way and not involving discretion. Second, some important Lloyd's brokers continued to object to divestment and their friends in the House of Commons slowed down the passage of the Bill. It eventually got to the House of Lords where delay through opposition again occurred. The Bill was finally passed into law on 25 July 1982.

Immediate after-effects of Lloyd's Act 1982

In the course of the struggle over the Fisher Report two associations were formed by the external members of Lloyd's, the Association of External Members of Lloyd's (AEML) and the less militant Association of Members of Lloyd's (AML). In the first elections for the new Council, which took place in November 1982, both bodies endorsed lists of eight candidates for the vacancies for external members. The AEML published a manifesto which it had difficulty in distributing as the Committee of Lloyd's refused to make available a list of the names and addresses of members. Eighty-three candidates stood. A number of underwriting agents took exception to the pledge in the AEML manifesto seeking to ensure that ownership and control of agencies be vested in the syndicate members. They accordingly refused to endorse any AEML candidates, and none were elected. Only two of the AML candidates were successful in the poll which was headed by Sir Marcus Kimball MP who had taken a prominent part in steering the Bill through Parliament. In December 1982, before the new Council came into office, it became known that the three nominated (or co-opted) members would be Sir Kenneth Berrill, chairman of a firm of stockbrokers and a former head of the government 'Think Tank', together with Mr Charles Gough, a senior accountant and Mr Edward Walker-Arnott, a solicitor with special knowledge of insolvency law. At the first meeting of the Council the existing Chairman and Deputy Chairmen were re-appointed.

Meanwhile the Committee of Lloyd's had appointed a score of working groups to consider and report on aspects of the Fisher recommendations in time for the new Council, when it met in January 1983, to take appropriate action, though it was not to be expected that all questions would be settled immediately.

One of the first tasks of the new Council was to set up the machinery provided in Lloyd's Act 1982 for the exercise of its disciplinary powers. The Act made it mandatory to establish a disciplinary committee and an appeals tribunal. The disciplinary committee contains a majority of the members of Lloyd's, though they are not necessarily members of the Council. The appeals tribunal has a president and a deputy president who, though appointed by the Council, must not be members of Lloyd's. The Council's role is that of setting up and appointing the two bodies, specifying the grounds on which disciplinary proceedings may be instituted and the penalties or sanctions that may be imposed. Thereafter the Council's disciplinary powers can be exercised only by the disciplinary committee and the appeals tribunal, except that the Council retains the power to confirm, modify or grant dispensation from any penalty or sanction imposed.

Lloyd's appointment of a Chief Executive is referred to in Chapter 15.

CHAPTER TEN

CENTRAL SERVICES

The central staff of Lloyd's has in the past been headed successively by a Master, a Secretary, a Principal Clerk and a Secretary General. The appointment early in 1983 of a Chief Executive, who has also become a member and a Deputy Chairman of the Council, was a belated recognition of the importance of Lloyd's central services to the welfare of Lloyd's. The Chief Executive lost no time in reviewing and reorganising staff responsibilities. These have been grouped into seven categories. The Secretary General, with the aid of appropriate departments, will service the Chairman, the Deputy Chairmen, the Council and the Committee of Lloyd's. He will also advise them of their powers and duties, thus fulfilling the secretarial function. There will be six group heads. The head of corporation services will be responsible for managing personnel, training, catering and the like with a temporary responsibility for the building redevelopment programme. A newly appointed head of finance will control the Corporation's finances, helping to formulate policies and assuming management responsibility for finance, accounts, investment and the internal audit. There will be a head of market services, a head of regulatory services, and a head of systems. Another new post, that of head of external relations has also been created. The appointee will carry responsibility for the information, legislation and taxation departments and will develop and direct Lloyd's public relations policy. To ensure co-ordination there will be a weekly meeting of the Chief Executive, the Secretary General, and the six heads.

Corporation Services Group

The Corporation Services Group includes a department dealing with the

Room, under the Superintendent of the Room, who ensures its smooth running with the aid of a staff of eighty-two including liveried staff. The Catering Department runs the Captains' Room and a complex of restaurants. The turnover in the basement complex alone comes to £1 million.

Personnel Department

The Personnel Department operates an enlightened policy for the recruitment and development of central staff. It concerns itself with career development and follows the principle of promotion from within as far as possible. An effort is made to provide a pattern of remuneration and benefits that is externally competitive and internally fair. The department operates consultative committees and induction procedures for new staff. Salary structures and administrations of pension schemes and staff benefits are among its responsibilities.

Training Department

Side by side with the Personnel Department is the Training Department which provides a group training scheme for the Lloyd's market. It caters not only for direct employees of Lloyd's, but for the whole Lloyd's community both in a training and advisory role. It does not seek to compete with the College of Insurance of the Chartered Insurance Institute in providing for education and training in specialist insurance subjects. Among its activities are induction, courses on the operation of the Lloyd's market for both underwriting and brokers' staff, Lloyd's documentation and short supervisory, management and communications courses.

Premises Department

The Premises Department is responsible for the management and administration of Lloyd's premises, whether owned or leased. The Department has divisions dealing with security and building services, and has responsibility for engineering and fire precautions. A section looks after the buildings at Chatham.

Purchasing Department

The Purchasing Department buys all corporation requirements except catering supplies, and controls stock held in stores. It spends more than £3 million annually.

Management Services Group

The Management Services Group comprises four departments whose work is described below.

Computer Services Department

The Computer Services Department provides data processing and on-line processing services for the Corporation and the market. A System Development Department has been redesigning the central accounting system and has been introducing membership computer systems to cover members' participation in syndicates and the monitoring of special reserve funds and central solvency system. The Department is responsible for the support and maintenance of all existing systems. It also has an O and M (Organisation and Methods) section and a section developing computer systems using small machines. It has begun to provide an information service about computer equipment and software.

Technical Department

The Technical Department provides support to production data-base systems and data-base design expertise. When new requirements arise for computer equipment or software the Department evaluates the options available and makes recommendations. It also performs a technical audit function.

Planning Department

The Planning Department sets computer strategy and oversees the operating plan. It maintains liaison with the market so that the market knows what is going on and new market requirements can be identified.

Communications Department

The Communications Department is responsible for providing and operating telecommunications services, both within the community and with the outside world. These include telephones, telex, radiopaging, facsimile image transmission and data communications, connecting terminals to computer systems and other data devices. A systems and communications policy board has responsibility for the departments concerned. It maintains links with the Lloyd's of London Press which is described below. The board spends about half its time considering possible future developments.

Finance Group

In addition to the departments below, the Finance Group operates an internal audit.

Finance Department

Prominent in the Finance Group is the Finance Department which has been concerned with the provision of financial services to the market.

Among these are the American and Canadian Trust funds which amount to over $4.6 billion, and the Late Settlement System related to the Terms of Credit Scheme, which provides information on settlements made by brokers to underwriters after the agreed settlement date, with a view to speeding up the process. The Department also provides money management services, for example, the profitable use of balances and the buying and selling of currencies. It is concerned too with the central accounting system, whereby all cash settlements are routed through the Central Accounting Office. The Department is also responsible for Additional Securities Limited, a wholly owned subsidiary of Lloyd's, which exists to provide insurance deposits in overseas countries where members of Lloyd's are licensed insurers.

Accounts Department

The Accounts Department at Chatham is responsible for all aspects of Lloyd's domestic accounting, including budgetary control and cash flow forecasting.

Investment Department

The Investment Department manages the investment of all funds under the control of the Corporation. It also advises on the acceptability of investments proposed by members for their own special reserve funds.

Taxation Department

The Taxation Department negotiates with national taxing authorities on points of principle and practice relevant to all Names. It provides the Inland Revenue with information required for calculating double taxation relief in the United Kingdom and is involved in the preparation and filing of tax returns in the United States and Canada for members not resident in those countries.

The Department also deals with the tax computations of Lloyd's, its subsidiaries and other funds.

Legal Department

The small Legal Department provides legal advice and assistance in respect of matters such as the admission of members and underwriting agents, problems (for example, over employment) arising within the Corporation, and the conduct of enquiries or disciplinary action. It advises on the use of outside legal advisers and works in conjunction with the Corporation's solicitors in any case. It advises on or assists in the conduct of any legal proceedings brought against or by Lloyd's in its corporate capacity.

Legislation Department

The Legislation Department has wide responsibilities. A stream of legislation all over the world affects the conduct of the insurance business. Insurers are increasingly regulated. There is the ever-present danger that legislation will be passed which may be workable for insurance companies, but not for the unique organisation of Lloyd's. The department seeks to learn at the earliest possible moment of what is contemplated in any territory, so that any necessary representations may be made before, rather than after, new legislation takes its final form. This form is more likely to be satisfactory if the legislators are informed in advance of the special features of Lloyd's. The aim of the department is to protect the freedom of Lloyd's underwriters to transact overseas business in one way or another as licensed insurers.

The Department has sections for the United States, Canada, Europe, the European Economic Community, including the United Kingdom, and the rest of the world. In the United Kingdom it is a comparatively simple matter to deal with the well-informed Department of Trade, but even within the United Kingdom, developments in Northern Ireland, the Channel Islands and the Isle of Man must be watched to ensure that Lloyd's position is not prejudiced. Similarly, proposed European Economic Community directives are subject to detailed analysis and the Department makes its views known through Lloyd's representation on the British Insurers' European Committee and the Comité Européen des Assurances. Whenever necessary, market associations are kept in the picture.

Much overseas business is conducted under licences issued by the states concerned, with a local attorney, who may be a lawyer or an accountant, appointed to accept responsibility for the observance of the licence terms. Documents will need to be filed. In some cases particulars of transactions are needed for taxation purposes. The technical section of the Department services the requirements for approval of underwriters under 100 laws. This involves statistical and other requirements, the calculation of deposits that may be required overseas, the payment of taxes and the annual filing of documents.

In addition to monitoring insurance laws all over the world, the Department examines proposed United Kingdom legislation of all kinds to see whether it would have a direct or indirect effect on the Lloyd's community.

Publicity and Information and Press Departments

The work of these Departments is monitored by an information policy board which meets weekly. Traditionally their task has been seen as

The caller's rostrum, from which the red-robed caller relays the names of brokers. The Lutine Bell is above.

photo: courtesy of Lloyd's

The Lutine Bell. Salvaged from the ship *Lutine*, which sank in 1799 and was covered by Lloyd's underwriters, it is a permanent feature of the Underwriting Room. It is struck on rare important occasions: once for bad news and twice for good.

photo: courtesy of Lloyd's

The *Hindenburg* in flames. The famous airship exploded over Airport Lakehurst at 18.15 hours on 20 May 1937, to the cost of Lloyd's underwriters.
photo: courtesy of BBC

An example of modern-day risk: the *Orion* oil-rig being towed in 1978. To cover the risk of such a large, expensive loss the insurance is spread over scores of syndicates.
photo: courtesy of BBC

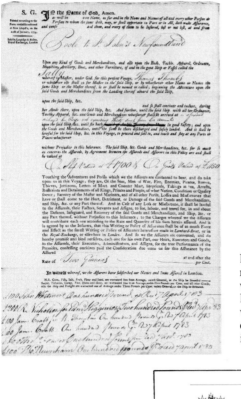

Lloyd's old and new forms of marine policy. The original wording was used throughout Lloyd's history until 1982, when the new, simpler form of marine policy was introduced.

photo: courtesy of Lloyd's

Lloyd's Marine Policy

We, The Underwriters, hereby agree, in consideration of the payment to us by or on behalf of the Assured of the premium specified in the Schedule, to insure against loss damage liability or expense in the proportions and manner hereinafter provided. Each Underwriting Member of a Syndicate whose definitive number and proportion is set out in the following Table shall be liable only for his own share of his respective Syndicate's proportion.

In Witness whereof the General Manager of Lloyd's Policy Signing Office has subscribed his Name on behalf of each of Us.

LLOYD'S POLICY SIGNING OFFICE
General Manager

This insurance is subject to English jurisdiction.

MAR

The front page of the earliest surviving copy of *Lloyd's List*, from 1740, and a more recent issue from 1983. *photo: courtesy of Lloyd's*

responding to requests for information and in this they have acquired a high reputation for helpfulness and objectivity. Lloyd's does not go in for collective advertising, but it produces booklets of high quality, welcomes visits from educational establishments and business organisations, and feeds information to the media in the United Kingdom by means of press conferences, handouts and responding to enquiries for information. For internal consumption, newsletters, *Lloyd's Log*, a house journal, and *Triangle*, a staff newspaper, are published. Articles and speeches are prepared. Documentary films have also been produced. It is fair to say that Lloyd's, with negligible expenditure on public relations, has long enjoyed esteem, and even affection. The past few years have been a stormy time for Lloyd's. The information service has risen to the occasion and has maintained its reputation for integrity.

Advisory Department

The Advisory Department exists to advise and assist the Council and the market on a wide range of subjects which can be grouped under three main headings. First, the Department operates regulations on certain topics of market interest. These include advertising, public policy, the war and civil war risk exclusion agreement, the extent to which financial and solvency business, which is subject to special conditions, can be transacted, and the classification of risks as between the various markets.

Second, the Department investigates all complaints received about Lloyd's. There are about 1,500 each year. It helps in settling domestic disputes without litigation which might lead to undesirable publicity. Arbitration is usually employed where an amicable settlement cannot be reached. It controls litigation against Lloyd's itself, as distinct from individual underwriters. Where underwriters are involved in litigation, consideration is given to the desirability of proceedings being heard in open court from the point of view of whether the good name of Lloyd's might be affected or the possibility of a judgment that might affect the interests of the market as a whole. The Department has no power to insist on its view, as underwriters are free to act as they think fit, but its recommendations are necessarily persuasive.

Third, the Department has investigated suspected insurance frauds involving business at Lloyd's or deceptive use of Lloyd's name. It deals with technical insurance enquiries, assists underwriters in the development of new forms of insurance and helps when difficulties or delays arise over the payment of premiums or claims.

In 1982 a spate of allegations over the conduct of certain underwriting agencies led to the normal procedure being bypassed by the appointment of special committees of enquiry, consisting of a senior lawyer and a senior accountant.

Membership Department

The Membership Department has three main areas of activity. First, in conjunction with underwriting agents it receives and vets applications for membership, operates the procedure for election, collects the deposit and oversees the transfer of the security into Lloyd's name as trustee for the member. Second, it is concerned with the underwriting arrangements of members, vetting applications for members to join (or leave) an agency or a syndicate or to increase premium limits, and monitoring members' means and premium incomes against premium limits. Third, the Department monitors the special reserve fund, consisting of members' money for which the Corporation is one of the trustees.

Computers are increasingly used in the work of the Department. They compile membership records and statistics, help to check that the activities of members comply with the rules and facilitate the monitoring of the interests of the beneficiaries of the trust funds.

Underwriting Agents and Audit Department

This Department has two distinct sections. The underwriting agents section is closely involved in the thorough review of the underwriting agency system which was recommended by the Fisher Report. A working party was set up in 1982 by the Committee of Lloyd's for this purpose. Some changes will in any case be necessitated by Lloyd's Act 1982. Meanwhile, the section operates the existing system. This entails vetting applications for the admission of new underwriting agents and ensuring that any conditions imposed are complied with. Once an agency has been admitted changes in partners, directors or shareholders all require approval. An annual check is carried out to ensure that the requisite errors and omissions insurance is being maintained. The section is also responsible for keeping underwriting agents under general review and for helping to settle disputes.

The audit section oversees the panel of auditors who conduct the audit of syndicates' accounts and verify the solvency of members. It has been involved with the preparation of an accounting and auditing manual. A computer system for dealing with the statutory solvency test was introduced in 1982. Audit (solvency) certificates must now be provided for all members of Lloyd's in respect of all the syndicates in which they underwrite. The section prepares and reviews the various forms which need to be lodged. The section is also responsible for monitoring reinsurance arrangements and syndicates' premium income. It deals with applications for the release of funds from trust accounts. It is responsible for calculating solvency margins and compiling returns for the Department of Trade, which, from 1 January 1983, entail the publication of more detailed revenue accounts and the phasing out of the former global statements which were all that was required of Lloyd's. If any member of Lloyd's is in default it is the audit section that advises whether claims should be met out of the Central Reserve Fund.

Brokers Department

The Brokers Department is concerned with the admission of applicants as Lloyd's brokers and with their continuing financial status and solvency. It monitors their compliance with requirements as to their own insurances, for example, against losses through dishonesty. It also ensures that the regulations relating to direct motor business transacted by non-Lloyd's brokers or agents are carried out. It watches over changes in the control of Lloyd's brokers, such as changes in group structure, boards or shareholdings. It deals with elections of annual subscribers and associates and the issue of complimentary tickets to the Room. The Department works closely with Lloyd's Insurance Brokers Committee.

Deposits Department

A large department is concerned with the administration of deposits at Lloyd's. Sections are concerned with the reception of new deposits, with changes to the underlying securities in any case, with the administration of the securities, as where there are rights issues or redemptions, and with cash transactions including the calculation and payment of interest to members. A control section operates a running audit.

Agency Department

The Agency Department dates from 1811. It is concerned with the appointment and control of Lloyd's agents who exist all over the world to provide intelligence, facilitate local surveys, and help, if called on, with the adjustment of claims on the spot. The Department not only recruits suitable agents, but records the facilities they offer, provides familiarisation courses for them in London, periodically inspects them and helps by providing them with any services or technical data they may require. Where necessary, it investigates complaints. For historical reasons the Settlement of Claims Abroad Office is part of the Agency Department. It handles claims adjusted by Lloyd's agents on Lloyd's policies and issues certificates enabling them to settle claims on the spot, where necessary putting the agents in funds for the purpose.

There is also a Salvage Arbitration branch. This branch is responsible for the Lloyd's Open Form of Salvage Agreement which is widely used for marine salvage work and pollution control. The agreement operates on a 'no cure, no pay' basis, thus eliminating the need for salvors to seek judicially a salvage award based on the value of the property concerned. Often ship-owners are called on for financial guarantees before their salvaged property is released. The branch may arrange for such guarantees in order to obtain release. On request it will provide for the appointment of arbitrators to determine awards.

Aviation Department

The Aviation Department was until 1959 part of the Agency Department. Its survey sections undertakes accident investigation with, in many cases, the assistance of Lloyd's agents on the spot. It monitors repair work and in its survey reports provides reserve figures for underwriters.

It undertakes preventive survey work such as safety studies. Its intelligence section is responsible for the *Blue Book* in loose-leaf form for updating. The *Lloyd's Confidential Record of Civil Aviation* is produced for the use of underwriters and brokers. The section also collects statistics and data for the market from governments and national registers of aircraft throughout the world, and provides details of relevant legislation. Publications include the *Lloyd's Aircraft Types and Prices* and the *Lloyd's Aviation Bulletin*.

Lloyd's of London Press

Intelligence gathering is an invaluable part of Lloyd's central services, with particular though not exclusive reference to marine insurance. The *Lloyd's Register of Shipping* is published by *Lloyd's Register* (described in Chapter 12) and so is not a publication of Lloyd's itself, though in recent years the computer-based shipping information resources of *Lloyd's Register* and the *Lloyd's of London Press* have been pooled. Lloyd's of London Press Limited is the publishing and intelligence subsidiary of Lloyd's. It receives information twenty-four hours a day, seven days a week, from the global network of Lloyd's agents and correspondents, and disseminates it in a wide variety of publications. On the marine side may be mentioned the *Lloyd's Shipping Index*, published five days a week and recording the movements of over 21,000 merchant vessels in the world. Then there is the *Lloyd's Voyage Record*, published weekly, which comprehensively covers the movements of vessels, changes in their status and casualties. The *Lloyd's Loading List*, also a weekly publication, provides an alphabetical list of ports throughout the world, with a list of vessels scheduled to sail from United Kingdom ports up to four weeks in advance. A Continental edition for exporters in Europe was introduced in 1978. Also available are the *Casualty Index*, *Lloyd's Weekly Casualty Reports* and *Lloyd's Monthly*

List of Laid Up Vessels. An important tool for marine underwriters is the *Confidential Index of Shipping* issued to subscribers only. This lists ship-owners' fleets, and attempts to show who is the real owner of a particular ship (as distinct from the nominal owner which is often a one-ship company) together with a casualty list in respect of each owner.

Lloyd's of London Press Limited is also noted for the *Lloyd's Law Reports*, a highly esteemed record of shipping and commercial legal decisions, and the *Lloyd's Maritime and Commercial Law Quarterly.* Other publications include marine atlases, year books such as the *Lloyd's Calendar*, and legal text books. Mention should be made of the *Lloyd's Survey Handbook*, first published in 1952, which is frequently updated and contains authoritative information on the nature and principal causes of loss or damage to commodities and the treatment available for such damage. A recent venture is the journal *Product Liability International.* Lloyd's of London Press Limited also runs a number of short conferences on shipping and insurance matters.

The Press is responsible for *Lloyd's List*, published six days a week with daily coverage of ships' movements, marine, aviation and non-marine casualties, labour disputes, port conditions and exceptional weather. World news is covered so far as concerns insurance, transport and industry. In recent years *Lloyd's List* has developed from an austere chronicle to a well-designed and readable newspaper, with a circulation of about 15,000.

Additional Securities Limited

One example of joint action in the interest of underwriters is Additional Securities Limited. Additional Securities Limited was formed in 1936 to enable deposits to be made with overseas governments, so that Lloyd's business might be transacted in the countries concerned. It was financed by a small levy on the premium income of non-marine underwriters and has succeeded in its purpose.

Lloyd's Syndicates Survey Department

Another example of joint action is Lloyd's Syndicates Survey Department, which surveys commercial and industrial premises proposed for fire insurance and provides reports, on the basis of which underwriters can assess the risk, rate the proposal for fire insurance and decide what safety measures are required. It employs some twenty surveyors.

Lloyd's Underwriters' Claims and Recoveries Office

Lloyd's Underwriters' Claims and Recoveries Office (LUCRO) provides an integrated claims service for Lloyd's marine underwriters in respect not only of marine claims but also of non-marine and aviation claims in which they are interested. The service grew piecemeal. In the late nineteenth-century it was confined to making recoveries on behalf of underwriters from third parties in respect of claims for which the third parties were liable. The claims office itself developed after 1916 when a start was made in centralising the service of policies and LUCO (Lloyd's Underwriters' Claims Office) came into being. Only in 1977 did the functions of negotiating and settling claims and making recoveries on behalf of underwriters coalesce into a single organisation.

The claims section is now used by most marine underwriters for both direct and reinsurance claims. It has subsections for hull, cargo and excess-of-loss reinsurance. The recoveries section acts both for Lloyd's underwriters and insurance companies at home and abroad. It exercises their rights against third parties on a 'no cure, no pay' basis, working closely with the cargo claims subsection and the Salvage Association. It also protects cargo interests when general average contributions are being assessed and in questions relating to salvage.

Lloyd's Policy Signing Office

Lloyd's Policy Signing Office, often known as the Bureau, has since its voluntary inception in 1916, come to occupy a central place in the operations of Lloyd's. Policies are in most cases, except in motor insurance, prepared and submitted by the broker concerned, together with the slip. The LPSO checks that the terms of the policy coincide with the terms of the slip. If not, the documents are returned to the brokers for correction. The policy is also checked to ensure that it complies with the requirements of the Committee of Lloyd's and of the relevant underwriters' association, also with market agreements and stipulations of the United Kingdom or foreign governments. If the policy passes these tests it is embossed with Lloyd's anchor mark and signed on behalf of the syndicates concerned. Each syndicate has a number and a distinguishing name or initials (known as its Pseudonym) allocated to it by the LPSO. A schedule of the syndicates involved and of their proportions is attached to the policy. The broker's slip is given a reference number and date and is returned with the policy to the broker.

The transaction is recorded for various purposes and a note sent to the underwriters and brokers. An advice card with details of the risk goes to the underwriters who are provided with information for statistical purposes. Accounting information is also sent both to underwriters and brokers and the transaction is processed through the central accounting scheme. An LPSO number indicates the currency and the type of transaction (whether it is cash or deferred). The LPSO date is the basis on which the month of settlement is calculated. The central accounting scheme issues accounts, and transactions in sterling are settled through it and the money distributed. Transactions in other currencies such as the United States dollar and the Canadian dollar are settled through the trust fund offices.

Syndicates may reinsure all or part of their business. The LPSO processes syndicate reinsurances, particulars of which are received through a broker in the form of debit and credit notes. They are checked by the LPSO which feeds the information into the central accounting scheme.

The LPSO participates in providing data for statistical purposes as required by the data processing department to provide statistics to other Lloyd's departments. It also participates in the Terms of Credit Scheme whereby maximum terms of credit are allowed to brokers, varying with various factors such as the country and whether direct insurance or reinsurance is concerned. Underwriters may negotiate periods of credit below the maximum. In special circumstances brokers may appeal to the Terms of Credit Tribunal for an extension of the period of credit. Each premium advice note issued by the LPSO indicates the period of credit allowed.

The LPSO operates various special schemes. In particular, the adjustable scheme applies where the first premium is a lump sum (known as a deposit premium) which is adjusted later by some variable factor, such as sums at risks periodically declared by the assured. The LPSO keeps details, reminds brokers when information is due and informs underwriters of outstanding items. Similarly, the contract scheme is used when a cover or line slip allows for the issue of policies of a defined class without prior reference to underwriters. Policies issued under this scheme are notified to underwriters in collective form on a single card issued each month.

The LPSO has a constitution of its own. At its head is a policy board comprising two representatives of the Committee of Lloyd's (one of whom is chairman), one representative from each of the four underwriting associations, and the general manager. Most of the work is now done at Chatham, but there is a London liaison office. The LPSO has a technical services group which issues a procedure manual and is constantly engaged in discussions aimed at developing procedures and documentation for the general good.

CHAPTER ELEVEN

MARKET ASSOCIATIONS AND MARKET AGREEMENTS

MARKET ASSOCIATIONS

Market associations at Lloyd's are a creation of the twentieth-century and have received little attention from writers on Lloyd's. Until 1909 the Committee of Lloyd's itself fulfilled the function of a market association, but with the growth of non-marine insurance, marine underwriters felt the need of a forum of their own for discussion of marine insurance topics. In 1909 they formed Lloyd's Underwriters' Association, which despite its name confined itself to the marine market. In the following year non-marine underwriters set up Lloyd's Fire and Non-marine Underwriters' Association. Fire insurance was then the dominant class of non-marine business, but the specific reference to it was later dropped and the title Lloyd's Underwriters' Non-marine Association assumed. In 1931 the volume of motor insurance and its special problems led to the formation of Lloyd's Motor Underwriters' Association. Four years later Lloyd's Aviation Underwriters' Association came into being in 1935, the year after the International Union of Aviation Insurance was established. The insurance companies were long without an aviation insurance association of their own. The Aviation Insurance Offices' Association did not come on the scene until 1949.

Lloyd's Insurance Brokers' Association (now the Lloyd's Insurance Brokers' Committee) was of an older vintage. It was formed in 1910, but at that time only a few brokers joined. The Association did not possess a separate secretariat until 1938. It was not until 1947 that all Lloyd's brokers became members.

The increasing importance of underwriting agents led in 1960 to the establishment of Lloyd's Underwriting Agents' Association.

The associations have developed with separate offices and secretariats. Each is governed by an elected committee of twelve to sixteen members. The chairmanship rotates. It is possible for someone to serve on more than one committee. For example, a marine underwriter may be on the committees of Lloyd's Underwriters' Association, Lloyd's Aviation Underwriters' Association and Lloyd's Underwriting Agents' Association.

Membership of the associations is not compulsory, but when the Fisher Working Party reported in 1980, all those eligible to join appeared to have done so, with the exception of one specialised syndicate in the marine market.

Lloyd's Underwriters' Association

The Association comprises Lloyd's marine underwriters. It acts officially for its members in technical aspects of their business. It is governed by a committee of fifteen members elected by ballot, plus the Chairman and Deputy Chairmen of Lloyd's, ex officio. The committee meets regularly to discuss underwriting and administrative problems affecting the variety of insurance effected in the marine market at Lloyd's. Questions often arise about foreign legislation, policy-signing, central accounting and the settlement of claims procedures. Market agreements may need to be hammered out for the smooth and efficient conduct of business. The Association also provides an information service for its members.

The Association works in close liaison with the company marine insurance organisations, the Institute of London Underwriters and the Liverpool Underwriters' Association. It nominates Lloyd's members to joint committees which deal with such matters as the drafting of policy clauses for the suggested use of insurers. It is also represented on the International Union of Marine Insurance.

Lloyd's Underwriters' Non-marine Association

This Association is concerned with all classes of non-marine insurance except aviation and United Kingdom motor. Its membership accounts for about half of Lloyd's premium income. It was formed for the purpose of 'meeting periodically to consider matters relating to fire and non-marine business at Lloyd's'.

Its membership comprises all the active non-marine underwriters at Lloyd's, currently numbering 109. There is a committee of twelve, plus the Chairman and Deputy Chairmen of Lloyd's and any non-marine underwriting members of the Committee of Lloyd's, ex officio. The committee meets twenty times a year and has numerous subcommittees. Its secretary has a staff of twenty-two.

Among the Association's tasks are to provide information to members, to help keep the doors of foreign markets open to Lloyd's, and to draft wordings for policy forms and clauses for the use of the market. Non-marine insurance is so disparate that there are over a thousand such wordings. Their use is not mandatory. Underwriters are free to use their own wordings. Brokers often put forward wordings of their own. Some contracts call for individual drafting to meet the insured's special needs. The Association recognises that contracts on specially worded forms probably outnumber those on the LNMUA forms. Nonetheless the existence of the LNMUA wordings is a great convenience to the market.

One service the Association has rendered its members for some years is to provide and keep up to date a volume containing all the market agreements affecting its member syndicates in the non-marine market. The Fisher Report commended this practice and recommended that other associations should follow suit.

Lloyd's Aviation Underwriters' Association

It was at the suggestion of the Committee of Lloyd's that three under-writers formed Lloyd's Aviation Underwriters' Association in 1935. Many matters were being referred to Lloyd's by the Air Ministry, the International Air Traffic (now Transport) Association and others. They needed expert consideration. From the start there was close co-operation with the Aviation Insurance Offices' Association, the corresponding company body formed in the previous year. The Joint Technical and Clauses Committee of the two associations is responsible for reviewing the policies and clauses used in the market. The LAUA has published a book of policy forms and clauses which is distributed world-wide.

The membership includes both specialist aviation underwriters and other underwriters who write aviation business. In January 1982 there were forty-one specialist members and thirty-four others. The Committee comprises ten specialist and two non-specialist members together with, as ex officio members, the Chairman and Deputy Chairmen of Lloyd's and any other specialist aviation underwriters who are members of the Committee of Lloyd's.

As well as informing members, the Committee has to devote much of its time to foreign legislation and developments in the international conventions governing the liability of air carriers. Attendance at inter-national meetings is often called for.

Lloyd's Motor Underwriters' Association

There were forty-six motor syndicates in 1982. Many have names such as HP, Red Star or Service, so that they look to the public much like insurance companies in their own right. A number are large syndicates with management structures like those of insurance companies and head offices at some distance from Lloyd's, which deal directly with brokers, both Lloyd's and non-Lloyd's.

The Association is an active one. Its committee meets once a fortnight. There are general meetings of the members in alternate months. The syndicates' claims representatives meet once a quarter to discuss matters relating to the handling and settlement of claims.

The Association was formed in the wake of the Road Traffic Act 1930, when it became apparent that many problems would arise for motor insurers because of the legal compulsion on a motorist to insure in respect of his third party liability for bodily injury. Over the years a system had to be devised for meeting the claims of injured third parties where for any reason an individual insurer was not liable to do so. The Association agreed in 1945 to the setting up of the Motor Insurers' Bureau for this purpose. It is a joint body of Lloyd's and insurance companies. Similarly, because motor vehicles cross frontiers, the compulsory insurance requirements of other countries have to be taken into account. After World War II the green card system was devised whereby an insurer in one country would supply a motorist with a card certifying that his vehicle had the necessary insurance cover in the country to which he was travelling.

The Association follows legal developments, co-operates in the working out of practical solutions to problems, and keeps its members informed.

An important consideration for underwriters in setting premium rates for a particular car model is its construction and the likely cost of repairs. Lloyd's motor syndicates have joined with insurance companies in financing the Motor Insurance Repair Research Centre at Thatcham in Berkshire, which examines and reports on new models and investigates repair costs.

Lloyd's Insurance Brokers' Committee

Lloyd's brokers are a species of the genus insurance broker, a fact that some of them recognised in helping to form in 1906 the first represent-ative body for insurance brokers, which later came to be known as the Corporation of Insurance Brokers. The Lloyd's Insurance Brokers' Association, set up in 1910, was at first little more than an advisory body which passed on to its members the requirements of underwriters. From the 1930s it assumed the role of representing Lloyd's brokers' interests to other collective bodies in the Lloyd's market and established links too with company organisations. In 1975–1977 it took a prominent part in the negotiations that resulted in the passing of the Insurance Brokers

(Registration) Act 1977. The broking profession needed unity and LIBA was one of the four bodies which set up the British Insurance Brokers' Council, soon to be turned into the British Insurance Brokers' Association. Despite the predominant position of Lloyd's brokers in the broking world, LIBA, in the interests of unity, was content to become one of the twenty-three regional committees of BIBA, as the Lloyd's Insurance Brokers' Committee. It thus has the use of BIBA's central facilities and at the same time operates autonomously in matters affecting the interests of members of the Lloyd's 'region' of BIBA, that is, *inter alia*, in all matters peculiar to their relationships in the Lloyd's community. There are sixteen committee members, from among whom a chairman and two deputy chairmen are elected annually.

The LIBC members also elect and appoint eight members (plus a chairman from the LIBC itself) to form executive committees for marine, aviation, motor and non-marine insurance. Through numerous technical subcommittees, the LIBC for Lloyd's brokers (and BIBA for all insurance brokers) provide a service on a wide range of matters, including re-insurance, legislation and office administration. Lloyd's brokers are represented on the British Insurers' European Committee, which deals in particular with the efforts to obtain rights for brokers to operate throughout the European Economic Community.

Lloyd's Underwriting Agents' Association

The approval of underwriting agencies and their registration has rested with the Committee of Lloyd's. In 1960 a need was felt by underwriting agents for a forum and a body which could speak collectively for them. Thus, Lloyd's Underwriting Agents' Association was formed. It maintains a liaison with the Lloyd's Membership Department and the Lloyd's Taxation Department and makes recommendations on matters affecting agents and the Names for which they are responsible. Its objects were expressed at the outset as to look after the interests of underwriting members and to examine and report on matters referred to it by the Chairman or Committee of Lloyd's. The Association has an elected committee of twelve members.

Associations and the Committee of Lloyd's

The market associations have in recent times assumed considerable importance, though they have hitherto had no formal place in the constitution of Lloyd's. There are many ways in which they are useful. In serving on committees individual members get training for future responsibility in the market. They benefit from liaison in technical matters with the insurance company market. The associations are well placed to obtain general agreement on some sensible course of action by members. They are a convenient sounding-board for the Committee of Lloyd's when it has been making policy. Membership of the Committee of Lloyd's and of the committees of the associations to some extent interlocks. The staffs of the associations are in close relations with the permanent staff of the Corporation. The Committee of Lloyd's has been able to leave to the associations many market matters which would otherwise have taken up its own time. In some matters, such as European Economic Community negotiations, where the outcome could affect in different ways both Lloyd's as a whole and the respective markets, the negotiations are conducted jointly by the Corporation and the associations.

All is not always roses. Demarcation disputes can arise, as happened in 1981 when Mr Ian Posgate, a marine underwriter, sought to lead a slip on the Qantas air fleet, whereas the aviation market took the view that it should have been led in that market. Further back there was the time when marine and non-marine underwriters developed separate policy-signing offices. The Fisher Report records that on occasion the Committee of Lloyd's has been frustrated in its desire to introduce reforms because not all the associations consulted have agreed and the Committee felt that it lacked the power to proceed in the absence of agreement.

MARKET AGREEMENTS

A feature of the associations is the informal way in which they work. It has been seen that membership is not compulsory. An association cannot enforce a market agreement. It has no disciplinary powers over its members. The Fisher Report saw no reason to give it any such power. The report hoped that the associations would continue to exercise their great moral influence over their members. In the last resort an association could refer complaints to the Committee of Lloyd's and the report recommended that it should be open to a disciplinary committee to take the view that persistent and deliberate breach of signed market agreements was a discreditable act or default.

Lloyd's underwriters are allergic to agreements of a tariff type that could restrict their freedom to write insurances on what terms they please. There are, however, many agreements or understandings that have been arrived at, by Lloyd's or by a section of the market, which restrict their freedom of action or provide that they must follow certain procedures. In some cases these agreements are enforceable by law, in others not. As an example of the first class, a motor syndicate wishing to write motor insurance in the United Kingdom must sign the Motor Insurers' Bureau Domestic Agreement. The Bureau is a body formed by insurers to provide funds to pay claims by persons injured in road accidents caused by motorists who ought by law to have insured their liability, but whose insurance is for one reason or another ineffective. By the agreement the syndicate accepts responsibility for paying its share of the cost of the Bureau's work. An example of the second class is the Joint Hull Understanding in marine insurance which lays down the procedure to be followed at the renewal of a marine insurance on ships.

Some classes of insurance are prohibited by Lloyd's and underwriters have to sign an undertaking agreeing not to transact them. In particular financial and solvency risks may not be insured, except for some kinds that specialised credit syndicates are allowed to underwrite. Reinsurances of approved insurance companies for financial and solvency risks are permitted. Sometimes it is not Lloyd's but underwriters as a whole who have agreed to a self-denying ordinance. An example is the War Risks Waterborne Agreement which precludes the underwriting of war risks on cargo in transit while it is on land, except in port, for fifteen days after arrival.

The regulatory authorities in some countries may require as a condition of Lloyd's doing business in the country that all underwriters shall observe certain agreements. The Chairman of Lloyd's may be required to declare formally that they have done so.

Many agreements are entered into by the underwriters in a particular market – marine, aviation, non-marine or motor. In some cases insurance companies are also parties to the agreement. Some of these agreements are purely procedural. The Underwriters' Agreement for Non-marine Insurance, for example, defines the circumstances in which brokers need consult only the leading underwriter about proposed changes to an insurance, without having to go to all the other underwriters. There are other agreements that simplify the processing of business. For example, there is a special procedure to deal with small items relating to claims, additional premiums and returns of premium whereby these are accumulated and settled periodically in bulk. Again there are agreements that certain types of claim where two insurers are involved shall be settled on some automatic basis without the necessity for argument between them over whether it is the insurer of one party or the insurer of the other who ought to pay. Such agreements save time and money. Many agreements simply put acknowledged market practices in writing.

The non-observance of some agreements could have a damaging effect on Lloyd's as a whole. For example, a breach of an undertaking in relation to insurance in an overseas country could lead to the withdrawal of Lloyd's licence there. In the case of many agreements the effect of a breach is to give an unfair advantage to the party in breach. The question of what disciplinary procedure should be applied to a breach or, worse, persistent breaches, is at present under consideration at Lloyd's.

To the extent that market agreements constitute restrictive practices they may require to be registered either in the United Kingdom or with the European Economic Community.

CHAPTER TWELVE

LLOYD'S AND THE INSURANCE COMPANIES

The 'love-hate' relationship between Lloyd's and the insurance companies is of long standing. Underwriting at Lloyd's breeds individualists, with each man relying on his own judgement and having to make quick decisions which may prove right or wrong, but which are essentially for the short term. If something goes wrong a syndicate can be dissolved and a new one formed for next year. Each man will be judged on his own performance. An insurance company, on the other hand, tends to greater caution. It will have to live with its decisions for an indefinite time-span. In underwriting it prefers a rating manual that can be administered by many people rather than rating by individual judgement alone. Whereas every active underwriter at Lloyd's has to exercise entrepreneurial qualities, an insurance company is likely to be staffed mainly by persons with an administrative bent. Entrepreneurs and administrators do not think in the same terms. Those in whom one set of qualities are highly developed are apt to be critical of the actions of others who do not share their predominant attitudes.

The historical relationship

Without enough of the entrepreneurial spark an insurance company can easily fall into torpor. In fire and life insurance, in particular, the rate book has for long been king. It was in marine insurance that Lloyd's underwriters and the companies first competed, from 1720 onwards. In the course of the eighteenth-century the two chartered companies, by a combination of caution and working according to rules, failed to make an important impact on the market. Often the rates they quoted priced them out of the market. By 1810 the chartered companies had only 4 per cent of the marine insurance market between them. A Parliamentary Select Committee said that two of the leading Lloyd's underwriters had as much business as the London Assurance.

The chartered companies and Lloyd's alike opposed the abolition of the companies' corporate monopoly of transacting marine insurance in 1810 and again in 1824. Neither of the parties saw any need to disturb the existing cosy arrangements. When the monopoly came to an end it was perhaps inevitable that the new companies should look to Lloyd's for their underwriters. The Indemnity Marine in 1824 recruited William Ellis, a young man who had worked at Lloyd's as assistant to his father who was an underwriter there. Even the Royal Exchange, when its marine underwriting ran into difficulties, went to Lloyd's to recruit an underwriter twice in the course of the nineteenth-century, in 1841 and again in 1880. One appointment proved successful and the other not. Marine underwriters traditionally get large remuneration if they are successful. At Lloyd's they take a commission on the profits and the Royal Exchange had to adopt this system in recruiting from Lloyd's. Henry Warre, who came in 1841, asked for £2,000 a year, a seat on the court of directors and a share in the profits ranging from 10 per cent on the first £15,000 to 2½ per cent on profits over £35,000. He was at first unsuccessful. He did not last long on the court and agreed to waive his right to profit commission on the understanding that the court would treat him generously in profitable years. They did, and in the last ten years of his sixteen-year tenure he received extra remuneration of £62,500.

The high income that a successful marine underwriter has always been able to earn is illustrated by the Thames & Mersey Marine Insurance Co. Ltd, founded in 1860. Its London underwriter was paid £5,000 a year and its Liverpool underwriter, taken from Lloyd's, £4,000. In contrast, the secretary at Liverpool, a practising barrister, received only £500 and the six clerks between £200 and £20 each. Even in more recent times the chief executive of an insurance company has found himself less well off than the marine underwriter.

In the marine market, where risks are often shared between Lloyd's and the insurance companies, co-operation for limited purposes has been common. The marine insurance companies paid Lloyd's a subscription for the shipping intelligence Lloyd's provided. Co-operation between Lloyd's and the marine insurance companies in the setting up of the *Lloyd's Register of Shipping* in 1834 and the Salvage Association in 1856 is described later in this chapter.

On the technical level, a fruitful century of co-operation between Lloyd's underwriters and marine insurance companies began in 1883 when a meeting of the underwriting community was held at Lloyd's 'to consider the details and phraseology of certain clauses usually inserted in Policies of Marine Insurance with a view to the general adoption of an established wording'. Before that, although both companies and Lloyd's had used the archaic Lloyd's SG form of policy (SG being the initials at the head of the policy standing for ship and goods), there were numerous variations in the clauses attached to it by various insurers. In the previous year the secretary of the Alliance Marine had compiled a book of the clauses used by the principal marine insurance companies. After the 1883 meeting, a number of Lloyd's clauses were adopted for general use. The association of marine insurance company underwriters, the Institute of London Underwriters (established in 1884), in 1888 adopted certain sets of clauses drawn from one of its member companies. These did not always follow the 1883 Lloyd's clauses.

In 1909 the Institute and Lloyd's underwriters formed the Joint Hull Committee to improve the state of marine insurance. Out of this grew agreements to limit the extent of over-insurance permitted on marine risks. The Committee also sought to regulate the procedure of underwriters at the renewal of hull policies and the Joint Hull Understanding was instituted whereby rates on renewal would not be arbitrarily cut without proper consideration of the previous experience. The Understanding has persisted, with occasional interruptions from 1921 to 1927 and from 1935 to 1936. It has been periodically revised and has proved pretty effective, though on occasion underwriters have resigned from the Joint Committee in protest at breaches of its terms by other underwriters.

An attempt to standardise cargo insurance clause wordings was made in 1908, but broke down. In 1912 the Institute produced suggested clauses for adoption. They were not found acceptable, but a drafting subcommittee was set up, consisting of two company underwriters, two Lloyd's underwriters, and two brokers, which provided two sets of cargo clauses which were adopted by the market in 1912. Nowadays, all clauses known as Institute Clauses are drafted by the Joint Technical and Clauses Committee, which still includes both company and Lloyd's underwriters.

Two examples of long-standing co-operation between Lloyd's and marine insurance companies are *Lloyd's Register of Shipping* and the Salvage Association.

From World War I to the present

In World War I the need was first felt for a body that could speak for insurance as a whole in discussions with government departments. Insurance companies were members of associations for the various classes of business. Two, the Fire Offices' Committee and the Accident Offices' Association, prescribed minimum rates to be charged by their members and therefore excluded from membership the so-called independent or non-tariff companies who had their own rating systems.

Other branches, the Institute of London Underwriters (for marine insurance companies), the Life Offices' Association and the Industrial Life Offices' Association, did not operate cartels and included most of the companies in the market. But the very existence of five company associations side by side with Lloyd's meant that government departments contemplating some legislative action had a lot of consultation to do before they could ascertain a collective insurance view. In 1916 a meeting was held to consider the formation of a representative insurance committee. Lloyd's was represented by Walter Faber, of the Lloyd's Underwriters' Non-marine Association. The outcome the following year was the establishment of the British Insurance Association, but by that time Lloyd's had withdrawn, so that the Association was one of companies only and it has so continued. The Association was restricted by its constitution to taking action only after its right to do so had been authorised by any sectional association concerned. It was not until after World War II that it started to play a leading role.

There were, however, occasions between the Wars when co-operation between insurance companies and Lloyd's proved useful. For example, when the Unemployment Insurance Act 1920 made unemployment insurance applicable to all industries, the Act permitted any industry to contract out of the state scheme if it could submit a scheme of its own to make more satisfactory provision. Only banking and insurance were able to submit schemes that satisfied official requirements. Over 300 Lloyd's underwriters and brokers came into the Insurance Unemployment Board, which operated successfully from 1921 to 1948 when the government ceased to allow contracting out of the state scheme. Lloyd's employers were represented on the board which charged contributions to employers only, so that insurance employees were covered without cost to them.

Similarly in 1937, joint action on the part of the BIA and Lloyd's was required to negotiate and bring into effect agreements whereby insurers agreed not to insure war risks on land and to limit the period during which marine insurers would cover cargoes against war risk after they were landed.

As mentioned in Chapter 11, both Lloyd's and the companies had to work together in 1945 in setting up the Motor Insurers' Bureau to provide for the collective payment of claims by injured third parties in road accidents, wherever for any reason the compulsory liability insurance that should have been effected was non-existent or inoperative. Insurers agreed to this as the price of avoiding government legislation on the subject.

Further instances of co-operation between Lloyd's and insurance companies since World War II are not hard to find. Three examples can be cited. Lloyd's underwriters have joined in supporting the Fire Protection

Association which was set up by the Fire Offices' Committee shortly after the War to advance the science of fire protection and to provide a service in preventing fires and controlling their effects. In 1957 the British Insurance (Atomic Energy) Committee was set up jointly by the insurance companies and Lloyd's to cope with the insurance problems arising from nuclear reactors. And the British Insurance Companies European Committee, formed by the companies to cope with their problems in doing business in Europe, has become the British Insurers' European Committee, with Lloyd's participation.

It remains true, however, that Lloyd's, while willing to co-operate in specific fields, has been jealous to maintain its independence of insurance companies. For example, a proposed take-over of C. E. Heath & Co. Ltd, the Lloyd's brokers, by the Excess Insurance Co. Ltd, with which it had close connections, was blocked in 1972 on the ground that Lloyd's and the insurance companies were antithetical. (*See* page 79 for further details.)

The fortunes of insurance companies and Lloyd's are locked together and for most purposes their interests are identical. Most countries have an organisation which can speak for insurers as a whole. The United Kingdom has as yet no such body.

Lloyd's Register of Shipping

The events leading to the establishment in 1834 of the *Lloyd's Register* are described on page 17. *Lloyd's Register of Shipping* has been separate from Lloyd's throughout its history. Its governing committee consists of nominees of Lloyd's, the marine insurance companies and ship-owners.

The *Lloyd's Register* of today has gone a long way from its origins, when it merely recorded information. The register of ships, published annually in July, is the world's only comprehensive record of sea-going merchant ships of 100 tons or over. It includes particulars of nearly 70,000 ships, of which more than 11,000 are 'classed' with the *Lloyd's Register*. New ships intended for such classification must be built under the Lloyd's registration special survey. The proposed plans and machinery have to be submitted for approval and the *Register's* surveyors keep a running check during the building period. The machinery is also constructed under special survey. Periodical surveys are carried out subsequently. Yachts and small craft may either be subjected to a full survey or may receive a Lloyd's Register Building Certificate, which does not entail subsequent periodical surveys. A register of yachts is published. Other publications include a register of off-shore units, submersibles and diving systems.

The *Register* has formulated rules and regulations for the construction and classification of steel ships and many other sets of rules, for example, for the carriage of liquefied gases in bulk, air cushion vehicles, floating docks, and inland waterways vessels.

The *Register*'s Research and Technical Advisory Services (RATAS) are in ever-increasing demand. For example, the Technical Investigation Department is available and will visit places where troubles are reported. The *Register* has a research department at Crawley with facilities for engineering, metallurgical and photo-elastic research. Quality control is undertaken for mass-produced products, with regular auditing of continuous production. Much survey work is carried out for the issue of statutory certificates, for example, on tonnage, load lines and safety.

The *Lloyd's Register* Industrial Services provide inspection, certification and other facilities in the non-marine field. Their activities are international. The Society was, for example, involved in early design studies for nuclear plant and works a great deal in hydro-electric schemes, both at fabricators' premises and on site. It has resident surveying staff in the world's industrial centres. It certifies freight containers and surveys container-handling equipment. There is a subsidiary authorised inspection agency for boilers and pressure vessels in the United States. Its services to the cause of engineering safety are widespread and comprehensive.

The *Lloyd's Register*'s full-time surveying staff numbers about 2,000. The *Register* now pools its computer-based shipping information with the Lloyd's of London Press.

The Salvage Association

In 1856 Lloyd's and the companies combined to form the Association for the Protection of Commercial Interests as respects Wrecked and Damaged Property. The body concerned is now called the Salvage Association. Its affairs are administered by a committee on which the Chairman of Lloyd's and chairmen of Lloyd's Underwriters' Association and Institute of London Underwriters sit ex officio, together with five nominees of each of the three bodies.

The Association is a non-profit-making body which supports itself from its fee income.

Nowadays, the Association has extended its powers to deal not only with matters affecting ships and cargo, but also those concerned with aviation and non-marine insurance.

The Association acts largely on the instructions of underwriters to investigate a casualty where a loss appears possible. It is not concerned with determining liability. Its task is simply to determine the nature, cause and extent of the damage and the best steps to be taken to repair or minimise the loss. This has led the Association into a variety of subsidiary activities, such as negotiating ship repair contracts, surveying and approving lay-up sites and approving towage arrangements and voyages for the purpose of fulfilling warranties under policies and for risk prevention. In modern times it has had to concern itself with oil rigs, pollution, nuclear and conventional power plant, pipelines, underwater cables, boilers and electrical plant.

The government of the *Lloyd's Register* and the Salvage Association has been shared between Lloyd's underwriters, marine insurance companies and merchants or ship-owners. The system of Lloyd's agents and the provision of marine intelligence has remained wholly in the hands of Lloyd's. The companies simply bought information by subscription. In 1871 a move was made to merge the Salvage Association with Lloyd's and to bring the insurance companies into the management of the combined institution. Discussions were entered into and in 1872 the Salvage Association came forward with a proposal for a general committee of Lloyd's to take over both the Association and the work of Lloyd's. The committee would consist of seventeen Lloyd's members, sixteen nominees of insurance companies and sixteen nominees of merchants or ship-owners. J. T. Danson, Liverpool underwriter of the Thames and Mersey, published a pamphlet which, after a good deal of abuse of Lloyd's, said arrogantly,

> You must immediately throw membership of Lloyd's open to the companies and hand over to the companies the right to elect one-third or more of Lloyd's Committee. That reform is essential if Lloyd's is to be allowed to continue. If you refuse you will be crushed and your news service taken from you.

Danson was doubtless influenced by the experience of the Liverpool Underwriters' Association, founded in 1802. In 1860 Liverpool had had a couple of hundred underwriters grouped in eleven syndicates and a score of partnerships transacting marine insurance and, usually, broking as well. The firms tended to form insurance companies after the Companies Act 1862 and the Association by 1872 was becoming company-dominated, which no doubt prompted the expectation that Lloyd's would take a similar path. The Committee of Lloyd's, however, drew back and reached a settlement whereby the companies joined an advisory agency sub-committee which kept them informed of all that was done about Lloyd's agents. The Salvage Association remained a joint venture.

CHAPTER THIRTEEN

LLOYD'S AND THE STATE

Lloyd's relations with the state have been on the whole amicable. As mentioned earlier, at the time of the Bubble Act 1720 underwriters were able to retain their rights to compete as individuals with the London Assurance and the Royal Exchange Assurance when those bodies were granted an exclusive right to transact marine insurance as corporations. From 1734 Lloyd's correspondents were allowed to send shipping intelligence free of postage to Lloyd's for publication in *Lloyd's List*. They simply addressed their letters to the Postmaster who immediately passed them on to Lloyd's. This privilege was continued when the first Lloyd's Agents were appointed in 1811.

Some difficulties arose during the eighteenth-century when the government was forced to legislate, first against gambling policies, then against the insurance of enemy property, and, at the end of the century, against insurance on the transport of slaves. All these measures were accepted and observed by much of the market with a good grace.

At the beginning of the nineteenth-century the proposed abolition of the exclusive rights of the London Assurance and the Royal Exchange Assurance was regarded by Lloyd's underwriters as a threat to the full rigours of competition. They therefore opposed the move and had to submit evidence to a parliamentary committee which reported in favour of opening the door to competition. Lloyd's was able to find friends, including some of its own members, among MPs, and successfully beat off the first attack in 1810. The door was not finally opened until 1824 in the face of a rearguard action.

The French wars had led to great prosperity at Lloyd's. The underwriters' lavish gifts to naval officers led to fears that officers would be affected in the performance of their duties by the hope of private reward (for example, in giving them a preference for the carrying of bullion), but the government took no action to curb Lloyd's activities in this respect. The Admiralty availed itself freely of the intelligence gathered by Lloyd's and was duly grateful.

Under Hozier's secretaryship (1874–1906) ties with the Post Office were successfully developed in the matter of signal stations. By the Lloyd's Signal Stations Act 1888 Parliament granted Lloyd's power to acquire land by compulsory purchase for the erection of stations. In 1901 the Admiralty and Lloyd's entered into a fifty-year agreement for co-operation in peace and war. The happy collaboration did not in the end extend to wireless, as in 1906 the Postmaster withdrew Lloyd's wireless licence, but Lloyd's signal stations continued to provide messages under a joint distribution service throughout the two World Wars and beyond.

State regulation of insurance

Governments everywhere have long been concerned with the protection of insurance policyholders, mainly against the possibility of an insurer's insolvency. Insurance is peculiarly open to abuse by unscrupulous persons who grant insurances, receive the premiums, and then fail to pay the claims. From time to time in earlier centuries some Lloyd's underwriters became insolvent and policyholders were unable to recover from them. As most Lloyd's policyholders were businessmen their plight did not cause many tears to be shed. It was otherwise with life insurance, not transacted at Lloyd's, where the insolvency of an insurance company could lead to distress among widows and orphans. Both Dickens in *Martin Chuzzlewit* and Thackeray in *The Great Hoggarty Diamond* wrote of fraudulent life insurance companies in the 1840s, but it was not until 1870, after the collapse of the Albert Life Assurance Company, which had absorbed a score of other offices, that Parliament acted and then only to a minimal extent. The Life Assurance Companies Act 1870 provided that the promoters of any new life insurance company must deposit £20,000 as an earnest of their good faith and that all life companies, old and new, must furnish annual returns and periodical actuarial valuations which the government would publish, thereby providing information from which a person intending to insure could choose his insurer. The principle was expressed as 'freedom with publicity'. The market remained open and free, but the facts were available to any who chose to ascertain them.

The 1870 Act applied only to life insurance. The forms of insurance transacted at Lloyd's were thus not affected. In 1906 Parliament passed the Workmen's Compensation Act 1906 which imposed on all employers, even private householders, a liability to compensate employees for injury in accidents at work. It was expected that most employers would effect insurance to cover their liability and the state became concerned

John Julius Angerstein (1735–1823). Often described as the 'Father of Lloyd's', his expertise established Lloyd's as the centre of marine insurance.

photo: courtesy of Lloyd's

Henry Montague Hozier (1838–1907). An energetic and able Secretary, he left behind him an efficient and comprehensive information network, and was one of the first to realise the potential of wireless telegraphy.

photo: courtesy of Lloyd's

Cuthbert Eden Heath (1859–1939). An innovative and resourceful underwriter, Heath expanded the range of Lloyd's non-marine insurance, and was always ready to accept a new, though well-calculated, risk. He became extremely wealthy.

photo: courtesy of Lloyd's

Peter North Miller,
Chairman of Lloyd's 1984.
photo: courtesy of Lloyd's

Ian Hay Davidson, Chief
Executive of Lloyd's.
*photo: courtesy of the
Financial Times*

A weekly meeting of the Committee of Lloyd's. The Committee is responsible, in brief, for admissions, security, provision of rooms, providing returns of business to the government and safeguarding Lloyd's and its reputation as a whole.

photo: courtesy of Lloyd's

Membership of Lloyd's includes many wealthy entertainers, sportsmen and sportswomen. Here, Henry Cooper is pictured with Bert Wigley, a waiter, at the Wharncliffe meeting in November 1980.

photo: courtesy of the Financial Times

with the potential ability of employers' liability insurers to meet claims. Accordingly the Employers' Liability Insurance Companies Act 1907 extended the principles of the 1870 Act to companies transacting employers' liability insurance. Two years later the Assurance Companies Act 1909 not only re-enacted the two earlier Acts, but added personal accident and fire insurance to the classes regulated. It called for £20,000 deposits from companies and £2,000 deposits from individual under-writers, but made an exception in favour of Lloyd's underwriters because Lloyd's was able to point out, first, that it already exacted deposits and, second, that it had taken measures in 1908 to ensure as far as possible, by imposing an audit on underwriters, that their solvency was being monitored. Parliament agreed that instead of requiring returns from each Lloyd's syndicate (as it did from each insurance company), a global return would be accepted from Lloyd's. In effect the government was delegating to Lloyd's the responsibility of regulating Lloyd's underwriters. This system of self-regulation has persisted from that day to this without detriment to policyholders.

Regulation was extended to motor insurance by the Road Traffic Act 1930 which imposed on motorists the obligation to insure in respect of their liability for bodily injury to third parties (*see* Chapter 11 for further details). Again the regulation of Lloyd's underwriters was left to the Committee of Lloyd's. The Insurance Companies Act 1946 substituted for the deposit system a requirement that general insurers should maintain a specified margin of solvency, that is, an excess of assets over liabilities. In this the government adopted the practice of Lloyd's since 1908, though Lloyd's, of course, also requires deposits.

Subsequent legislation, arising out of repeated failures of insurance companies, has strengthened the powers of what is now the Insurance Division of the Department of Trade and Industry to control insurers. The most serious failure in the post-war insurance world was that of the Vehicle & General Insurance group in 1971, when some 800,000 motor policyholders found themselves without cover overnight. A tribunal of inquiry found that certain civil servants, including the Under-secretary responsible for regulation, had been negligent. There was a general tightening up and further legislation ensued in 1974.

Lloyd's and the European Economic Community

By this time the United Kingdom had joined the European Economic Community and efforts were being made to harmonise the law of insurance regulation in the countries of the Community. The Treaty of Rome of 1958 postulated a free market throughout the community in goods and services, including insurance. This would mean in principle that anyone living in the Community should be free to insure with any insurer operating in the Community, but freeing the market was subject to the condition that distortions of competition should first be eliminated. It would clearly be a distortion if some insurers were subject to more restrictions by their governments than insurers in other countries. Regulatory practices varied considerably among the countries in the Community. At one extreme, the West German government exercised control over policy wordings, some premium rates, and the investment policy of insurance companies. At the other extreme, as has been seen, the United Kingdom exercised no such control. A programme for progressively bringing about a free market in insurance, which was adopted by the European Commission in its early stages, visualised that full freedom would be attained by 1969, but full freedom is still not yet in sight.

It has been found necessary to segment the problem and to deal with each segment separately. Reinsurance was the first part to be solved (in 1964), but as reinsurance had always been more or less freely available across frontiers this was no great advance. As for direct insurance it became necessary to consider life and general business separately and then, in both cases, to seek freedom for insurers in one country of the European Economic Community to set up branches or establishments in any other such country. These establishments would then be required to operate within the framework of the national regulatory body concerned. Directives providing for freedom of establishment were issued for general insurance in 1973 and for life insurance in 1979.

Freedom of establishment however means little for Lloyd's under-writers whose primary operation is London-based. What they would like to see is freedom of services, that is, freedom for insurers, whether companies or individual underwriters, to transact their business across frontiers. It is this freedom that remains obstinately out of sight. There are a series of obstacles in the way. Three examples will illustrate the difficulties. First, countries that charge a tax on insurance premiums fear that the tax will be liable to evasion if insurances are effected outside their jurisdiction. Second, the law relating to insurance contracts differs from country to country and some countries fear that their own citizens might find their claims denied by foreign insurers on a ground that would not apply within their own country. (Attempts to harmonise insurance contract law have been drawn out for a long time, but are so far fruitless.) Third, countries that require policy wordings to be submitted for government approval are not prepared to allow insurers operating overseas the freedom to issue policies in unapproved wording.

No doubt there is local resistance from insurers in some countries to seeing their domestic markets disturbed by competition. In Luxem-bourg, for example, insurance brokers have not been permitted to operate, and Lloyd's relies on brokers for its business. The European

Insurance Committee, speaking on behalf of insurers generally, has expressed itself in favour of freedom for insurers, but difficulties persist. It is perhaps salutary to remember that even in the United States after 200 years of independence, each of the states has its own laws regulating insurance and an American insurance company established in one state may not be free to operate in others.

In all the negotiations with the European Commission representatives of Lloyd's have had to concern themselves with the shape of the proposed regulations to ensure that they are suitable not only for insurance companies, but for Lloyd's own special constitution. This involves explaining the constitution to the officials concerned in each country, so that they appreciate that if one syndicate establishes itself in a country it does so for its own purposes and does not act for Lloyd's as a whole. It is necessary to appoint someone in the country to accept responsibility for the syndicate's affairs and to receive service of process. Policies may be required to specify that local law should apply. Negotiations are necessary to ensure that local regulations are adapted to fit Lloyd's business. In France, for example, Lloyd's has to maintain an office, not to obtain insurance business, but to record details of policies written in that country.

Negotiations with foreign countries

Lloyd's is of course no stranger to the need for negotiations with foreign countries. Its Legislation Department has these as its full-time job. For many years Lloyd's resisted pressure to make local deposits in order to carry on insurance business, but it was fighting a losing battle. How the battle was lost in Illinois and what steps Lloyd's subsequently took to provide deposits are described on page 23.

Relations with Parliament

With the British Government Lloyd's relations have continued to be excellent, whichever party is in power. Wealthy MPs of all parties have been underwriting members. Lloyd's has often been successful in negotiating favourable taxation arrangements, for example, the abolition of stamp duty on marine insurance policies. Lloyd's was excluded from the operation of the Policyholders Protection Act 1975 which placed an obligation on insurance companies to meet from a levy the claims of private policyholders and, in some cases, of third parties who were affected by the failure of an insurance company. Lloyd's is consulted before regulations under the Insurance Companies Acts are promulgated, to ensure that the arrangements proposed are workable for Lloyd's. If anything, the government has been too considerate. In particular for a long time it did not require that returns of Lloyd's premiums should be in the same form as those for insurance company premiums (the former have been stated net of commission, whereas the latter are expressed gross). This made the work of comparison difficult. The Insurance Companies Act 1974 had to be modified by the Lloyd's (Financial Resources) Regulations 1981, for example, for the purpose of calculating the solvency margin which insurers are required to show. The regulations provide that Lloyd's net premiums shall be increased by a percentage specified by the Department of Trade in the light of the most recent statistical data. Steps have recently been taken to render Lloyd's and companies' returns more easily comparable.

Some conclusions

The main object of state regulation of insurance is to guard policyholders against the risk of an insurer's insolvency. In this respect the combination of Lloyd's internal arrangements and statutory requirements has been completely successful. What is not clear is the extent to which underwriting members are protected against sharp practices by Lloyd's underwriting agents or underwriters and brokers to whom they entrust their capital. The events of 1981–1982 appear to show that their protection has been inadequate. It is in this respect that self-regulation needs to justify itself. With the changed constitution of Lloyd's brought about by Lloyd's Act 1982, the Council's new powers and the appointment of a chief executive of suitable calibre, the prospects are encouraging.

CHAPTER FOURTEEN

LLOYD'S GREATEST MEN

Many remarkable men have worked at Lloyd's. To some of them Lloyd's nowadays awards its Gold Medal for services rendered. Three men stand out: they are John Julius Angerstein, Henry Hozier, and Cuthbert Heath. Their claims to greatness are very different.

John Julius Angerstein (1735–1823)

The first, John Julius Angerstein, is often described as the 'Father of Lloyd's'. He came of a family of German merchants who traded with Russia, some settling in that country, where Angerstein was born. At the age of 15 he was sent to England and apprenticed to Andrew Thompson, a Baltic merchant. At 21 he entered Lloyd's as a subscriber. In the following year he became a junior partner in Dick & Angerstein, insurance brokers, in Cowper's Court off Cornhill. He changed partners from time to time. In 1783 his firm Angerstein, Crokatt & Lewis had its office over the Royal Exchange. He also engaged actively in underwriting and traded as a merchant. His businesses prospered.

Angerstein had been one of those who broke away from the old Lloyd's in 1769 to join the new Lloyd's. He first came to general notice when, four years later, after the Committee had failed to find adequate premises, he obtained a lease of rooms in the Royal Exchange for Lloyd's at a favourable rent. He agreed to take the lease before he had the Committee's formal approval. Thereafter he was elected to the Committee and served as Chairman in 1786, from 1790 to 1796, and again in 1806. Many achievements are attributed to him. For example, in 1794 when a number of Dutch and Russian ships insured at Lloyd's were seized by enemy governments, Angerstein bought the salvage rights; two years later he succeeded in recovering the ships' value. He obtained, despite opposition, an Act of Parliament which prohibited ship-owners from changing the name of a vessel as had often been done in the past with intent to mislead underwriters. In 1795 he persuaded the government to make a loan of exchequer bills for the temporary relief of trade. He also devised a scheme of state lotteries which the Government adopted. Later, at his instigation, Lloyd's offered £2,000 for the design of a secure lifeboat.

In 1807 as a broker he succeeded in placing the largest insurance ever written up to that time – £656,800 on treasure in the *Diana*. To this total the two marine insurance companies contributed only £25,000 and Angerstein had to seek individual underwriters high and low, not confining himself to Lloyd's.

Angerstein's commercial and financial activities brought him a fortune. Despite the prejudice against those engaged in trade he gained entry to the highest society. He was a friend of Johnson, Garrick, Reynolds, Pitt and George IV. He corresponded with Nelson. Angerstein is best known to the public for his collection of fine pictures which he assembled with advice from Sir Thomas Lawrence and Benjamin West. After his death, thirty-eight of his pictures were bought for the nation, at the suggestion of George IV, and with other pictures were exhibited to the public at Angerstein's Pall Mall house, on the site of the present Reform Club, pending the construction of the National Gallery. William IV donated a striking portrait of Angerstein by Lawrence, who also painted Angerstein's second wife, alone on a desolate island without hat or shawl.

Angerstein's last service to Lloyd's was given at the age of seventy-five, when he appeared in 1810 before the Parliamentary Committee which was considering a petition to allow a new insurance company to compete with the London Assurance and the Royal Exchange Assurance. He was an impressive witness, brushing aside the complaints of some that insurance was hard to obtain at times and that policyholders suffered from the occasional insolvency of individual underwriters. Such insolvencies, he claimed, were rare and could be avoided by the use of an experienced broker. The monopoly was not ended until a year after his death.

He retired from Lloyd's in 1811 and lived till the age of eighty-eight. He was a public figure and was caricatured by Gillray. Twice married, to widows, he had a son and a daughter by his first wife.

A far-sighted entrepreneur with a golden touch, Angerstein took the view that good underwriting would drive out bad and that losses through the periodical failures of individual underwriters were too rare and too small to trouble about. Policies subscribed by him were known as Julians after his second forename and were in demand because of the security the name offered, at least for his own share. The Napoleonic Wars were the golden age of marine insurance. Angerstein exploited them to the full, though a former partner of his as a broker for fourteen years, in evidence to the Committee of 1810 denied that broking was a passport to riches, and claimed that he could afford no more than one domestic servant.

Angerstein has been described as 'easy and unaffected in manner, hospitable and unostentatiously generous – could hold his own in conversation modestly'. He was known for practical philanthropy. He helped to relaunch the Veterinary College which had got into financial difficulty, and interested himself in the welfare of boy chimney sweeps. In his later business life he rode for an hour or so before breakfast at 10 a.m., leaving for the City at 11 a.m. and returning soon after 5 p.m. In the autumn he hunted for two months in Lincolnshire.

Henry Montague Hozier (1838–1907)

In 1874 the Committee of Lloyd's appointed Captain Henry Hozier as secretary to the Corporation. He was born in 1838, the youngest of eight children of an advocate at the Scottish Bar who came of a well-known Glasgow family. Hozier was educated at Rugby and the Edinburgh Academy. He entered the army and distinguished himself, passing first in and first out of the Staff College. He served in China and Abyssinia, and was attached to the German Army during the Franco-Prussian war of 1866, which he reported for *The Times* as military correspondent. During the Franco-Prussian War of 1870 he was assistant military attaché to the Prussian Forces and was decorated with the Iron Cross. His service led him to write half a dozen books. At the age of thirty-two he had become controller at Aldershot.

Hozier was a forceful, fiery and ambitious man, more successful in his career than in his private life. His first wife having divorced him, he married at the age of forty a daughter of the Earl of Airlie whom he subsequently divorced. One of his children by his second marriage was Clementine, who married Winston Churchill. Hozier's allowance to his second wife was grudgingly paid and at one time he allowed it to fall into arrears. At another, it is said, he attempted to kidnap one of his daughters who was living with her mother. He deleted all reference to his marriages from his entry in *Who's Who*.

But whatever his private life he was an outstanding servant of Lloyd's. He appears to have dominated the Committee in an unprecedented way. No doubt this was all the easier because the Chairman during most of his tenure as Secretary until 1906 was an outside grandee.

Hozier's management style was autocratic, with a parade-ground manner. He drew a heavy line between officers and men but was good at picking subordinates. He lost no time in making himself felt. Within a week of his arrival he submitted suggestions for the better management of Lloyd's. Under him the Committee found that it was not called on to adjudicate on the multiplicity of questions that arise when a secretary is weak.

The Committee evidently appreciated his services. Hozier's salary on his appointment was £1,000. Eight years later the Committee doubled it and gave him, besides, 500 guineas as a mark of its appreciation.

Hozier came into office soon after Lloyd's Act 1871 had given the Corporation a constitution which was to survive almost unchanged for forty years. He was therefore spared constitutional controversies until the rise of non-marine insurance towards the end of the century. It was no part of the Secretary's duty to concern himself with underwriting. The underwriters themselves took care of that. What he could do, and did do, was to concentrate on the efficient running of the central machinery for the benefit of underwriters. Perhaps the most important area of central activity was the provision of shipping intelligence. In the army Hozier had concerned himself actively with intelligence. He therefore approached this duty with interest and knowledge. He had a special interest in science at a time when communications were developing scientifically.

In his earliest years at Lloyd's Hozier saw the desirability of having telegraph stations at strategic points on the coast to report shipping movements. He acquired numerous sites for this purpose. In 1884 he claimed that more than 90 per cent of ocean-going vessels bound for the United Kingdom were reported on by a Lloyd's station before their arrival in port. By then Lloyd's had seventeen stations at home and six abroad. By the Lloyd's Signal Stations Act 1888 Lloyd's obtained compulsory purchase powers over land for signal stations. Hozier worked in harmony with the Admiralty. In 1901 a fifty-year agreement for co-operation was signed.

This agreement came just at the time when wireless telegraphy was developing. Hozier had interested himself in this from the first and had even invented some workable apparatus. He became a director of one of Marconi's companies and obtained a government licence for five Lloyd's stations to operate a wireless service from ship to sea. At some stations Lloyd's transmitted all kinds of messages, not merely shipping intelligence, on behalf of Marconi, but the arrangement did not work well and was terminated in 1906 with litigation in which Lloyd's lost the day. The Postmaster-General withdrew Lloyd's wireless licence and criticised in Parliament some figures produced by Hozier. Hozier, incensed, challenged him to a duel. The duel did not take place.

Meanwhile Hozier had been under attack by a member of the Committee of Lloyd's (later its Chairman) who complained of extravagance. It appears that £140,000 had been spent over the years on signal stations, including £25,000 on Hozier's own extensive travels. Lloyd's intelligence services certainly raised the Corporation's international prestige even if, for the direct purposes of underwriting, they were dearly bought. That the price was not thought too high seems to be indicated by the action of Lloyd's in electing Hozier to honorary membership on his retirement in 1906 at the age of sixty-eight. It was an honour rarely granted.

Hozier's reign is also noteworthy for the introduction in 1880 of a system for paying cargo claims abroad, at first in India, China and Australia, and later extended elsewhere. But for this Lloyd's would have been hard put to it to compete with insurance companies who already paid claims abroad through their local branches and agents, whereas at Lloyd's the tradition had been for all settlements to be made in London.

Hozier maintained wide social and political connections. He sought election to Parliament, unsuccessfully contesting Woolwich as a Liberal-Unionist in 1886. He was knighted in 1903. He died in 1907, a year after his retirement, while visiting a signal station at Panama. His legacy to Lloyd's was the well-chosen staff he left behind him which enabled his less high-powered successors to cope with the many problems of the following decades.

Cuthbert Eden Heath (1859–1939)

Cuthbert Eden Heath was born in 1859, one of a family of seven. His father, who later became Admiral Sir Leopold Heath, destined him for the services, but the deafness which he suffered as a child diverted him to business. Leaving Brighton College at the age of sixteen he spent two years in France and Germany to learn languages and then entered the firm of Henry Head & Co., underwriters and brokers at Lloyd's. In 1880, as soon as he was twenty-one, he joined an underwriting syndicate with the aid of a loan of £7,000 from his father. In the following year he started a syndicate of his own. Marine insurance was the dominant business of Lloyd's at the time, but Heath also early interested himself in the incipient non-marine business. In 1885 he agreed to reinsure the fire business of the Hand in Hand Office, the oldest fire insurance company, which was being refused reinsurance by the tariff insurance companies because it distributed its profits to policyholders. (His father was a director of the Hand in Hand.)

Heath was an imposing figure. He stood six feet, two inches high and carried a hearing aid in a black box. He adopted a sympathetic approach to underwriting and was therefore popular with brokers. When shown a novel risk his reaction was 'why not?' and he therefore accepted risks that other would shun, though he always based his terms on a careful analysis. He was the first to insure household burglary risks and he soon extended the cover he offered to 'all risks', including accidental loss, at a suitably high rate. Soon he offered 'all risks' cover to reputable jewellers in the form of jeweller's block insurance. He was also willing, as tariff insurance companies were not, to insure against loss of profits through fire. By 1887 he was underwriting for a syndicate of fifteen members and was a recognised leader in the non-marine insurance market. By the end of the nineteenth-century he was actively writing hurricane and earth-quake insurance, having characteristically first made a careful study of the records of such natural disasters over a long period.

One step led to another. To get more business he established a firm of insurance brokers, C. E. Heath & Co. Ltd in 1890. By 1894 Heath was writing nearly £100,000 in premiums for his own syndicate. He wrote also for other syndicates on a profit commission. But he needed more capacity. At this time the Committee of Lloyd's still had reservations about non-marine insurance. The deposits of members were considered to be for the security of marine insurances only and non-marine policies did not bear the anchor, which since Lloyd's Act 1871 had been the hallmark of a Lloyd's policy. Heath pressed the Committee to accept deposits from members in respect of non-marine insurance, but the Committee declined. He hit on the device of forming an insurance company (the Excess Insurance Co. Ltd), with a paid-up capital of £5,000 which reinsured two members of his syndicate. There seems no doubt that Heath underwrote for the Excess in his box at Lloyd's, contrary to one of the fundamental rules of Lloyd's, enshrined in Lloyd's Act 1871. When taxed with this in 1909 Heath claimed that he had not read the rules until a few months previously. Be that as it may, Heath was always urging steps to increase the security of Lloyd's underwriting. He took the lead in inducing members to accept an audit of their accounts as evidence of their solvency and carried his point about this in 1908, thereby anticipating a requirement for deposits in the Assurance Companies Act 1909.

Heath continued to innovate. One new form of insurance was that of trade credit, started by a company in a small way in 1893. It needed reinsurance. Heath, when approached at Lloyd's, declined to lead on the slip, but said he would follow if another underwriter led the slip, and did then accept a line. When the company got into financial difficulties in 1896, from a cause unconnected with credit insurance, Heath helped to form the Trade Acceptance Guarantee Syndicate of Underwriting Members at Lloyd's. In 1903, after the original company had passed into the hands of the Commercial Union, Heath bought its business for the Excess where it remained until 1918 when it was transferred, with the Excess underwriter, to a new company formed under official auspices: the Trade Indemnity Company, with Heath as chairman. In 1923 Heath clashed with the Chairman of Lloyd's over a proposal that credit insurance should cease to be transacted at Lloyd's. The following year a compromise was reached which permitted underwriters to reinsure, though not directly to insure credit risks. The Trade Indemnity Company was strengthened with extra capital from six large insurance companies and C. E. Heath & Co. Ltd., and Heath remained as chairman. He continued for the rest of his business life to take a special interest in credit insurance and at the age of sixty-nine was the president at an international credit insurance meeting in Paris.

Heath was also prominent in satisfying the demand for employers' liability insurance which mushroomed after the passing of the Workmen's Compensation Act 1906. The queue at his box in the Room lengthened to inconvenient proportions.

He is credited with being the first to write excess-of-loss reinsurance on fire risks in the United States soon after the San Francisco earthquake and fire of 1906, when reinsurance was in great demand. Under an excess-of-loss treaty the reinsurer pays only for losses that exceed a stated minimum. Similarly he embraced without hesitation the so-called Carpenter Plan of 1926, whereby a reinsurance contract premium is based on the cumulative experience of the ceding insurer, without the need for elaborate particulars of every insurance transacted, as had been the rule before.

Heath early interested himself in motor and aviation insurance. His syndicate issued a policy on a steam car in the United States in 1907, and in 1919 he formed, with Sir Edward Mountain of the Eagle Star, the British Aviation Insurance Association. He did not, however, make striking progress in either field.

His principal services to Lloyd's were in providing new forms of insurance, developing the American market, and getting new safeguards as to the financial security of underwriters. He took the lead in forming the Lloyd's Underwriters' Non-marine Association in 1910, though he seldom attended its meetings. In 1911 he was elected to the Committee of Lloyd's at the top of the poll and served for four years, though with decreasing activity. During his term C. E. Heath & Co. Ltd sponsored an American broker for membership of Lloyd's. The application was rejected. It was fifty years ahead of its time.

In World War I Heath wrote much insurance against air raid damage. He calculated systematically the chances of loss and multiplied the probability by six 'to be on the safe side', as he said. He served on a government committee which worked out a successful scheme for the government itself to operate.

Heath early became a wealthy man. His wife entertained lavishly. At his country house in Surrey he employed fifty domestics. He was generous in charity. In 1918 he became joint master of the Surrey Union

Hunt. Heath was made an OBE in 1920. He served as High Sheriff of Surrey in 1925 and later as Deputy Lieutenant. Lloyd's honoured him by having his portrait painted to hang in the Committee Room, side by side with Angerstein and three other worthies, in his Deputy Lieutenant's uniform.

As a man he was gentle in manner and popular with his staff. He had an eye for talent. Always modest, he drew admiration for his business ability and personal qualities, though his deafness prevented him from shining in company. Outside his underwriting he showed a vagueness about money that characterises some rich people. He was once heard to remark that however much he gave away, it did not seem to make any difference. He certainly gave to Lloyd's more than he took.

CHAPTER FIFTEEN

THE BUSINESS OF LLOYD'S
AND ITS FUTURE

Lloyd's has taken a buffeting since 1975. Its troubles have arisen partly from the state of the world, which is in recession, and partly from its difficulties in enforcing internal discipline. Recessions pass, but while they last underwriters are bound to suffer from having to reduce their rates if they are to retain their share of the world's insurances in the face of protectionist restrictions overseas and increasing competition for the world's available business, which can hardly grow in a no-growth world economy.

Changing world insurance markets

The United States is Lloyd's principal market. Nearly half of all general insurance business in the world is transacted in the United States. Voices there have long been raised against the export of insurance premiums. Except in Illinois and Kentucky, Lloyd's is debarred from playing a direct part in the market, except for what are called excess and surplus lines, that is, insurances that cannot be placed on satisfactory terms with the companies licensed to do business in the state concerned. Much American business reaches Lloyd's by way of reinsurance. American insurers have in recent years become much more international in their outlook, partly because they are called on to cater for the insurance needs of large multinationals, so many of which are American in origin. To the extent that Americans can obtain cover in their domestic market for risks both at home and abroad they will have less need to look to Lloyd's. The American insurance community naturally likes to keep all the business it can at home. Hence the foundation of insurance exchanges at New York and in Florida and Illinois. The Florida exchange chose a former secretary of the Lloyd's Insurance Brokers' Association as its chief executive and Lloyd's firms are participating in syndicates of the New York exchange. It is too early to say how far these exchanges will succeed, but whatever success they have is bound to be partly at the expense of Lloyd's.

The formation of international reinsurance corporations and pools in Arab countries, the Far East and other parts of the developing world could also in the long run lessen the demand for reinsurance in London, but it could be in the very long run. The Lloyd's market cannot at present complain of any lack of business on offer. The current problem is rather over the adequacy of rates that underwriters can obtain and this reflects the current world over-supply of insurance. Unless economic growth has suffered a stop rather than a check there seems no reason to fear that Lloyd's will go short of business. At the same time Lloyd's share of world-wide, non-life insurance business shrank over the years 1950–1979 and the trend looks likely to continue downwards.

Developments in communications technology

One problem that Lloyd's faces in the immediate future is the new communications technology that can be introduced to facilitate the business of Lloyd's. At present there is hardly a computer terminal to be seen in the Room and the capacity of the existing electricity system would in any case preclude their use on a large scale. All this will change when Lloyd's is installed in its new premises in 1985. In 1981 Lloyd's appointed a Systems and Communication Board which has reported on plans for future communications systems in the market. There are two tasks. First, systems have been redesigned to replace the central accounting system, to cope with syndicate reinsurance and subsequently with statistics. This work is due for completion in 1983. Second, there is a need to consider how far technology can help in other work, such as the relationship between members, underwriting agents and syndicates. Micro-computer systems have been introduced for the Finance Department and the Brokers Department and word-processing office systems have also been adopted in London and Chatham. The main need is to consider comprehensively what will be wanted for the future by underwriters and brokers. The Florida Exchange has already adopted a system (the SOLAR system) which, it is claimed, will provide for all accounting, underwriting, claims, administrative and management information requirements in a combination of on-line, real-time and batch processing, with potential remote access and the ability to offer risks by electronic mail. No doubt it is easier to adopt such a comprehensive system when one is starting an exchange from a green-field site. For Lloyd's the question is rather how fast one can proceed into the electronic age with the general agreement that will be necessary from a

market which deals in widely disparate risks with varying requirements. Does the coming **revolution** threaten the time-honoured
procedure whereby typed slips **are** taken around the Room by brokers
who queue more or less patiently to see underwriters? Cannot many
transactions be completed by messages from one computer terminal to
another? The Lloyd's of 1983 is not vastly different from the Lloyd's of
1783 in its way of doing business. It is unlikely that the underwriters and
brokers of twenty years hence will operate in the same leisurely way.

Changes in Lloyd's internal structure

Lloyd's difficulties over internal discipline have arisen through many
causes. The first, ever present, is the financial greed of a few people and
their willingness to cut corners, if not to act with downright dishonesty,
to achieve an above-average profit for themselves. Wrongdoing has
occurred in every age and cannot be altogether eliminated. One can only
hope for comprehensive rules, adequate policing, and effective
sanctions. The time has passed when the governing body of Lloyd's, in
the name of personal freedom, could ignore the shortcomings of
individuals and shrug off the consequences of misbehaviour. In stages
over the centuries the Committee has devised a set of provisions which
have proved effective in protecting policyholders from loss by the default
of underwriters. They have been less successful in protecting the Names
themselves.

The official line has always been that Names know the risks they run
when they lay out their money at Lloyd's, one of the risks being the
conduct of their underwriting agents. They must stand by the
consequences of having made a poor choice of agent. This would be more
plausible if the Names had access to full information about the various
underwriting agents in the market and so could make an informed
choice. In fact such information has not been freely available in the past.
More of it is now obtainable, thanks to the initiative of those who have
been organising representation for the Names, but even the publication
of summaries of underwriting agencies' accounts does not ensure that
full comparable financial information is available. The accounts of some
agencies are not promptly filed. Different agencies have used different
financial conventions. And where, as often happens, the financial affairs
of an underwriting agency are mixed up with those of an insurance
broker, the allocation of costs or the basis of charging costs to the
underwriting agency has often been obscure. Similarly the Name has
little material on which to judge the charges he is asked to pay the
underwriting agent or the terms of sub-agency agreements. The majority
of the Fisher Working Party considered that all Names for whom an agent
acts should receive the same treatment, but this has not always been so.

There have been complaints of delays by agents in paying Names the money due to them. It also appears that where a Name has been introduced, a continuing commission has been paid for the introduction. The Fisher Report considered that all Names should be entitled to know the amount of any introductory commission. This is already mandatory for American Names.

Dissatisfaction over the losses sustained by members of the Sasse syndicate led to the formation of the Association of External Members of Lloyd's. Some members of the Association soon broke away. A further body, the Association of Members of Lloyd's, was formed. The Association of Members has published a league table showing the profitability of syndicates in the various markets in recent years. The table, although incomplete, is said to cover 80 per cent of Lloyd's total premium income.

Although no doubt most Names are fairly treated by underwriting agents, there is scope for increased regulation to ensure, first that Names have adequate information to make an informed choice and, second, that a standard of conduct is prescribed for underwriting agents, so that possible abuses of their power do not occur. The new Council of Lloyd's, with its provision of the separate representation of External Names, should ensure that this desirable state of affairs is soon brought about.

In 1982 a number of cases arose of allegations that reinsurance had been siphoned off from syndicates on terms intended to profit reinsurers connected with the Managing Agencies of the syndicates. It was even alleged that in some cases the reinsurance premiums ended up in the hands of companies owned wholly or in part by directors of the broking groups which also controlled the Managing Agencies concerned and that their personal interest in these transactions had not been disclosed. The Department of Trade has ordered an investigation into the affairs of two of the largest groups of Lloyd's brokers and there have been resignations from their boards meanwhile. It will take some time for the full truth to emerge. If it should appear that the Names have been unfairly treated, not to say swindled, a demand is bound to grow for a better system than self-regulation, as it has operated in the recent past.

The compulsory divestment by insurance brokers of their interests in Managing Agencies will occupy a lot of attention over the next five years. From time immemorial underwriting and broking have gone hand in hand at Lloyd's, so that the operation of separating these mature Siamese twins will not be without its difficulties. These should not, however, be magnified. For most brokers the operation of underwriting agencies yields only a small proportion of their profits. Again, brokers will be able to continue to operate as Members' Agents. It is to be expected that many Managing Agencies will be acquired either by Names or by the agencies' own employees, or a combination of the two. Their total value has been estimated at something between £75 million and £150 million.

Even when brokers have divested themselves of the ownership and control of Lloyd's underwriting agencies they will not be divorced from insurance company underwriting. Insurance brokers have long acted as underwriting agents for insurance companies, especially overseas companies, who want a footing in the London market. The large insurance brokers own or have substantial holdings in insurance companies which may give them effectual control. They argue that where they are instructed to place a large risk, it is reassuring to other insurers if the brokers retain some of the risk in their own insurance company, thus demonstrating the brokers' belief in the soundness of the insurance and the adequacy of the premium. So far there has been no move to require brokers to divest themselves of such company underwriting interests, though the Howden affair, where Lloyd's syndicates controlled by Howden are said to have reinsured with Sphere Drake, a company in the Howden Group, may cause further consideration of existing practices. In October 1982 *The Times* reported an interview with Sir Peter Green, Chairman of Lloyd's, in which he pointed out that Lloyd's was concerned only with the Lloyd's activities of the Group, its Lloyd's broker companies and its two Lloyd's underwriting agencies. 'Everything else that Howden does', he went on to say, 'is nothing whatever to do with us in the sense that we have any power to regulate them.'

In the sphere of self-regulation there is much unfinished business at Lloyd's. For example, the Corporation has not so far succeeded in preventing syndicates from exceeding their allotted premium income limits. In theory responsibility rests with each member for keeping within his personal limit and he is subject to sanctions if he does not. In practice he can only discharge this responsibility by relying on his underwriting agent. Although the then Chairman of Lloyd's in 1979 considered that over-writing could not always be avoided, the Fisher Report was insistent that further steps needed to be taken to avoid it as far as possible. There are various ways in which difficulties can arise. For example, premiums only get into the calculation of premium income when the policy has been entered at the LPSO and the premiums paid; when interest rates are high, brokers have an incentive to delay submission of documents. Again, premium limits apply to premiums net of reinsurance, without regard to the quality of the security offered by the reinsurer. The Fisher Report recommended that consideration should be given to applying limits to the gross, rather than the net, premiums. This would certainly facilitate the task of ensuring that limits are observed. The report recommended that disciplinary proceedings should be taken against underwriting agents or active underwriters where limits are persistently exceeded.

Another problem is that of brokers who exceed their terms of credit given by underwriters. The amounts outstanding are persistently high. Lloyd's in 1975 instituted a system of monitoring brokers' performance. Where the performance is unsatisfactory the brokers have been interviewed by a Deputy Chairman, but no sanctions have hitherto been imposed, such as publishing the names of defaulters or imposing payment of interest on overdue balances. Late payment of accounts is a running sore in the relations between insurers and brokers. It is an area in which self-regulation has so far proved ineffective. As the Fisher Report piously remarks, 'It would be to the general advantage if a fair system could be devised for improving the speed with which brokers and underwriters settled accounts.' Underwriters, it is true, have not always been free of blame for delay in the settlement of claims. Settlement delays are not peculiar to Lloyd's, or even to insurance. Barristers persistently complain of delay in the receipt of professional remuneration. The fact is that barristers are dependent for their income on receiving briefs from solicitors and therefore hesitate to complain to the Law Society as they are entitled to do. Similarly it may be supposed, many underwriters are reluctant to take action against dilatory brokers, and all the more if brokers are large and therefore powerful.

Now that half the business of Lloyd's is in the hands of three broking groups, the problem of broker power can only be intensified. The Fisher Report dealt rather lightly with the concentration of broking business. It pointed out that only large brokers were able to provide the technical expertise necessary for handling many large risks. Large brokers had done much to promote the interests of Lloyd's and to market its services. At the same time it found that further concentration might be a threat to Lloyd's and recommended that the Council of Lloyd's should take power to prescribe that future mergers should be subject to its prior approval. Similarly it proposed that the Council should have power to limit the size of underwriting syndicates if necessary to avoid serious prejudice to Lloyd's or Lloyd's policyholders.

Lloyd's has too long suffered from the British disease of apathy towards change until change is forced upon one. An organisation that worked pretty well when Lloyd's was regarded as a club in which most of the active members knew one another and reliance could be placed on their observance of the rules, written or unwritten, proved ill adapted to cope with a vastly increased scale of operations. The evils that have arisen through the remoteness of underwriting members and their lack of control of those whose duty it is to look after their interests should be cured by the new constitution which Lloyd's Act 1982 provides. In some quarters resistance to change persists. One has only to cite the dogged resistance of certain brokers to mandatory divestment of their Managing Agencies, which delayed the passing of the Act; the failure in 1982 to command a sufficient majority for the expulsion of a member; and the election to the Committee for that year of a prominent underwriter, who eleven years earlier had himself been suspended. It will take strong central direction to ensure that all the necessary reforms are carried through.

It is no derogation of Lloyd's central staff to say that its authority has needed strengthening. For too long there has been a tradition of recruits joining at an early age for a lifetime as club servants. The Cromer Report is said to have recommended the appointment of a chief executive of 'director general' rather than 'secretary general' calibre. If so, its recommendation was not adopted. Twelve years later the proposal for a chief executive was revived.

In January 1983, at the insistence of the Governor of the Bank of England, the Council decided to appoint a Chief Executive at a salary reported to be £120,000. Mr Ian Hay Davison, senior partner of Arthur Andersen & Co., the accountants, and chairman of the accountants' Accounting Standards Committee was accordingly appointed. He was also elected a Deputy Chairman. The idea of a high-powered executive was resisted in some quarters at Lloyd's, but pressure for the appointment could not be withstood. It remains for the new arrangement to be made to work.

The central staff of Lloyd's has four main functions. First, it runs the market and this it performs admirably. Second, it provides intelligence to the market and information to the public. The intelligence work is first-rate. The information service is quick, willing and imaginative, but is hampered by a tradition of confidentiality of documents which is at times nonsensical. One need only cite the unwillingness to issue the report of the *Savonita* inquiry to the press at the same time that it was published in *Lloyd's List*, the refusal to provide particulars of the membership for circulation purposes in the 1982 elections to the Council, and the reluctance to publish particulars of the financial results of syndicates and underwriting agencies.

The third function is regulation of the participants in the market. The staff has succeeded in its task of protecting policyholders. Much less has been done to protect the Names. As the Fisher Report pointed out, regulation by undertakings which apply to some and not to others is an unsatisfactory method and difficult to administer. It should be somebody's job to devise systems that can be worked.

This brings us to the fourth function, that of planning for the future. It is here that the great weakness of Lloyd's is found. The staff and the Committee have been so busy with their day-to-day work and with plugging leaks when they arise that evidence of forward planning has seldom been apparent.

The history of Lloyd's resounds with the banging of stable doors after the horse has escaped. Recent history is no exception. The Corporation has been a ship with a frequently changing master (the Chairman) and a willing crew, but little provision for keeping a look-out to avoid the rocks ahead.

The objections in theory to the historic structure of Lloyd's are manifold. The concept of personal unlimited liability for businesses in which one invests capital has long given way everywhere else to that of the company with limited liability. Breaking down all transactions into tiny fractions has practical disadvantages as well as advantages. A Central Reserve Fund has been found necessary, but it cannot be used for the benefit of the Names. As the Fund is intended for the protection of the public one would expect its value to be published; but it was kept secret until 1983. It amounted then to £120 million.

It is possible for one syndicate on a Lloyd's policy to decline liability for a claim when others are willing to pay. From the policyholder's point of view a single insurer would in principle be preferable for this purpose.

The recently formed American insurance exchanges operate on the principle of limited liability. In theory such a system could be devised for Lloyd's, but in practice its introduction would raise many difficulties. At the time of the Cromer Report in 1970, which recommended the admission of limited companies as underwriting members, the difficulties (for example, over taxation) were considered insuperable. There is no reason therefore to expect a radical reconstitution of Lloyd's.

Table 15.1 Overseas Earnings of United Kingdom Financial Institutions

	£ million					
	1976	1977	1978	1979	1980	1981
Insurance	806	913	1,039	1,009	860	974
Banking	382	315	671	167	314	1,329
Commodity trading etc.	309	230	295	298	340	360
Investment trusts	47	51	52	58	82	91
Unit trusts	11	12	15	22	33	39
Pension funds	14	17	24	46	87	107
Solicitors	29	36	44	52	61	67
Brokerage	198	212	228	313	347	457
Lloyd's Register of Shipping	17	21	20	18	19	28
Total	1,813	1,807	2,388	1,983	2,143	3,452
Insurance as per cent of total	44.4	50.4	43.5	50.4	40.1	28.2

Source: The Pink Book, HMSO.

The importance of insurance in general, and Lloyd's in particular, to the United Kingdom national economy cannot be overlooked. Table 15.1 shows the overseas earnings of United Kingdom financial institutions for the years 1976–1981. Insurance regularly accounts for 40 to 50 per cent of these earnings. Table 15.2 shows the proportions of insurance overseas earnings attributable to Lloyd's and to brokers, who are principally Lloyd's brokers, for the same period. Table 15.2 amply demonstrates the importance of Lloyd's activities to the United Kingdom's balance of payments. Periodical Labour Party proposals for taking parts of insurance into public ownership have skirted around Lloyd's. Any threats from that direction appear remote.

Table 15.2 Overseas Earnings of Insurance 1976–1981

	£ million					
	1976	1977	1978	1979	1980	1981
Insurance companies	300	326	377	357	276	290
Lloyd's	336	382	425	424	341	382
Insurance brokers	170	205	237	228	238	302
Total	806	913	1,039	1,009	855	974
Lloyd's and brokers as per cent of total	62.8	64.4	63.7	64.6	67.4	70.2

Source: The Pink Book, HMSO.

Lloyd's has shown great resilience in the past. Under its new constitution there seems no reason why, despite the shocks of 1982, it should not continue to flourish, even if its share of world insurance slowly declines. To do so it will need to increase its vigilance in internal affairs. Lloyd's must seek to anticipate, rather than simply react to, future events. Passivity must give way to initiative.

BIBLIOGRAPHY

Brown, Antony. *Cuthbert Heath* (David & Charles, Newton Abbot, 1980).
Brown, Antony. *Hazard Unlimited* (Peter Davies, second edition, 1975).
Bruce, G. *Poland's at Lloyd's* (Henry Melland, 1979).
Catchpole, W. L. and Elverston, E. *BIA Fifty 1919–1967* (British Insurance Association, 1967).
Cockerell, Hugh and Shaw, Gordon. *Insurance Broking and Agency – the Law and the Practice* (Witherby, 1979).
Chartered Insurance Institute. *Study Course 312 – Management Part II Lloyd's* (Chartered Insurance Institute, 1981).
Flower, Raymond and Wynne-Jones, Michael. *Lloyd's of London – an Illustrated History* (Lloyd's of London Press, second edition, 1981).
Gibb, D. E. W. *Lloyd's of London – a Study in Individualism* (Macmillan, 1957).
Golding, C. E. and King-Page, D. *Lloyd's of London* (McGraw-Hill, 1952).
Grey, H. M. *Lloyd's Yesterday and Today* (Syren and Shipping, third edition, 1926).
Hogsflesh, G. W. 'The Marine Market Today and Tomorrow', *Journal of the Insurance Institute of London* 44 (1955–1956).
Insurance Institute of London. *Institute Cargo Clauses, Report H. R. 5* (Insurance Institute of London, second edition, 1964).
Insurance Institute of London. *Institute Time Clauses – Hulls, Report H. R. 3* (Insurance Institute of London, 1963).
Insurance Unemployment Board. *1921–1948 Insurance Unemployment Board* (Insurance Unemployment Board, 1948).
John Holman & Sons Ltd. *John Holman & Sons Ltd* (undated).
Keir, David. *The Bowring Story* (Bodley Head, 1962).
Lloyd's Act 1871.

Lloyd's Act 1888.

Lloyd's Signal Stations Act 1888.

Lloyd's Act 1911.

Lloyd's Act 1925.

Lloyd's Act 1951.

Lloyd's Act 1982.

Matthews Wrightson Group. *Irons in the Fire* (privately printed, 1952).

Maufe, G. *et al.* 'A Short History of Willis Faber & Dumas Ltd', *Willis Faber & Dumas Group Review* (Summer 1970 and Summer 1971).

Soames, Mary. *Clementine Churchill* (Cassell, 1979).

Supple, Barry. *The Royal Exchange Assurance – a History of British Insurance 1720–1970* (Cambridge University Press, 1970).

Thames and Mersey Marine Insurance Co. Ltd. *Thames & Mersey Marine Insurance Co. Ltd 1860–1960* (privately printed, 1960).

Wright, C. and Fayle, C. E. *A History of Lloyd's* (Macmillan, 1928).

GLOSSARY

Active underwriter. The person who acts on behalf of a Lloyd's syndicate in accepting insurances.

Agent. A person with authority from another, the principal, to act on his behalf within the terms of his authority.

All risks insurance. Insurance of property against loss or damage however caused, subject only to stated exceptions.

Allocated premium limit. The amount up to which premiums may be accepted on behalf of an underwriting member of Lloyd's governed by his means and the amount of his deposit.

Anchor policy. A policy bearing Lloyd's trade mark, the anchor.

Annual subscriber. A person, usually the director or senior employee of an insurance broker, who is entitled to enter the underwriting Room at Lloyd's without being a member.

Associate. A person admitted to the underwriting room at Lloyd's without being a member or an annual subscriber, because his work is for the benefit of the market.

Assurance. Same as *Insurance.*

Assured. Same as *Insured.*

Assurer. Same as *Insurer.*

Audit, The. Examination by accountants of the records of an underwriting member or syndicate to check that the financial position is in order and that Lloyd's regulations have been complied with.

Average. In marine insurance, loss or damage.

Average adjuster. One who assesses and apportions losses in marine insurance.

Binding authority. An authority by an underwriter to an agent to grant cover on the underwriter's behalf and to prepare and issue evidential documents.

146

Box. An underwriter's seat and desk at Lloyd's.

Captive insurance company. An insurance company formed by a trading company, a trade association or the like, primarily for the insurance of the founder's own risks.

Cedent. An insurer who transfers risks by means of reinsurance.

Central accounting system. A clearing-house system operated by Lloyd's for sums due from underwriters to brokers and vice versa in respect of premiums and claims.

Closing. Completion of an insurance by a broker after a slip has been subscribed.

Consequential loss insurance. Insurance against pecuniary loss, other than material damage, resulting from an insurable peril such as fire.

Contingency insurance. Insurance against relatively remote possibilities.

Co-ordinating agent. An underwriting member of Lloyd's who transacts business through two or more underwriting agents is required to nominate one of them to co-ordinate the allocation of his premium limit.

Coverholder. An agent authorised by an underwriter to grant cover on the underwriter's behalf.

Credit insurance. Insurance for creditors against their inability to collect debts owed to them.

Cross-risks. Marine insurance on voyages between ports outside the United Kingdom.

Deductible. Same as *Excess.*

Disclosure. The legal obligation on one proposing for insurance to disclose all material facts that he knows or ought to know about the risk proposed.

E and O cover. Errors and omission cover, that is, professional indemnity insurance.

Excess. The level up to which an insured (or reinsured) bears his own loss.

Excess of loss reinsurance. Reinsurance which covers losses only to the extent to which they exceed a stated sum.

External member. A member of Lloyd's who is not a *Working member.*

Facultative/obligatory. Applied to a reinsurance treaty where the original insurer has the option whether to reinsure a particular item, but the reinsurer is obliged to accept what is offered.

Facultative reinsurance. The reinsurance of a risk where the original insurer may elect whether or not to offer it to a reinsurer and the reinsurer is free to accept or reject it.

Fringe company. A company, other than a major British company, by whom or on whose behalf insurance is written in one of the underwriting rooms near Lloyd's.

H/C. Held covered (pending completion of an insurance).

Honeycomb slip. A slip with a honeycomb of boxes in which the numbers of Lloyd's syndicates on a risk are inserted, used when special agreements are added to an initial slip.

IBNR. Losses under an insurance that have been incurred, but not reported.

IBRC. Insurance Brokers' Registration Council.

Incidental non-marine. Insurances written by a marine underwriter as an adjunct to his marine insurance account.

Indemnity. The legal principle whereby the insured under a property or liability insurance is entitled to have his loss made good but no more.

Inland marine. A category of marine insurance relating to inland water and inland transit risks, extended in American practice to the insurance of some classes of property on land.

Insurable interest. A legal requirement that, for an insurance of property (or liability) to be valid, the insured must be so related to the subject-matter that he would benefit from its survival or suffer from loss or damage to it.

Insurance. A contract whereby one party, the insurer, in return for a premium, undertakes to pay to the other party, the insured, a sum of money or its equivalent in kind upon the happening of a specified event which is contrary to the insured's interest.

Insured. One who effects an insurance.

Insurer. One who grants an insurance.

Jewellers' block insurance. The insurance of the stock of a jeweller against all risks, with certain exceptions.

K and R. Kidnap and ransom insurance, whereby, if a person is kidnapped, the insurer will refund ransom paid.

Leader. An active underwriter whose judgement of a class of risk is so respected that other underwriters are likely to follow his syndicate (which appears first on a slip) in accepting a share of the insurance.

Line. A share of an insurance accepted by a syndicate. The amount the underwriter has agreed to accept when signing a slip is known as the written line. The amount eventually insured by the policy is known as the signed line.

Line slip. A *Signing slip* issued off a long-term cover.

Lloyd's broker. A partnership or company permitted to broke business at Lloyd's.

Lloyd's Central Fund. A fund held by Lloyd's to protect policyholders in case any member cannot meet his underwriting liabilities.

Lloyd's Name. An underwriting member of Lloyd's who at the time of his election is a United Kingdom resident and has been employed for five years with an underwriting agent or with Lloyd's brokers, either at Lloyd's or in their London or main administrative office on insurance work relevant to Lloyd's.

LPSO. Lloyd's Policy Signing Office, a central bureau for the signing of Lloyd's policies.

Managing Agent. An underwriting agent who manages one or more Lloyd's syndicates.

Marine insurance. The insurance of ships, cargoes and freight and of installations such as oil rigs.

Market agreement. An agreement subscribed to by all underwriters in a given section of the Lloyd's market.

Market association. An association of these engaged in some particular trading activity at Lloyd's, eg. marine underwriters or underwriting agents.

Means test. An evaluation of the assets of a person to determine his eligibility for underwriting membership of Lloyd's.

Members' Agent. An underwriting agent who acts for a member of Lloyd's in all respects except managing the syndicate he joins.

Name. An underwriting member of Lloyd's whose name appears on the list of those participating in a syndicate.

Non-marine. The term applied to all insurances at Lloyd's other than marine, aviation, motor and life insurances.

Non-underwriting member. A member of Lloyd's (for example, a retired underwriter) who is not empowered to underwrite.

Off slip. A slip used for the noting of further items arising out of the original slip.

Open policy. A cargo policy designed to cover shipments as and when declared.

Open slip. A slip covering a sum sufficient to provide for a number of shipments to be advised as they take place.

PAN. Premium advice note.

P and I club. A mutual association of ship-owners for the purpose of insuring its members. P and I stands for protection and indemnity.

Personal reserve. A fund retained by the underwriting agent in the premiums trust fund on behalf of an underwriting member.

Pooling. A system whereby a number of cash items or insurances or reinsurances is placed in one fund to be subsequently shared out among the members of the pool in agreed proportions.

Portfolio. The total business of an insurer.

PPI. Policy proof of interest. Under a PPI policy the underwriter waives his right to require the insured to prove his insurable interest.

Premium. The amount paid to the insurer for an insurance.

Premium trust fund. A trust fund into which all premiums are paid, to be used for the settlement of claims.

Proportional reinsurance. Reinsurance in which the reinsurer accepts an agreed proportion of the original insurance.

Pseudonym. An abbreviation or combination of letters used in Lloyd's practice to identify a broker or underwriting syndicate.

Quota-share reinsurance. Reinsurance in which the reinsurer accepts a stated proportion of every original insurance of a defined class.

Quotation slip. A slip whereby an underwriter offers to accept an insurance on the terms stated in it without either party binding himself to immediate insurance.

Reinsurance. Transfer of all or part of the risk assumed by an original insurer to another insurer, called the *Reinsurer.*

Reinsurance to close. Reinsurance effected at the end of a three-year account, so that the account may be closed and the ultimate profit or loss determined.

Reinsured. An insurer who cedes insurance by way of reinsurance.

Reinsurer. An insurer who accepts reinsurance business from another insurer.

Retention. The amount of an insurance retained by an insurer after he has effected reinsurance.

Retrocession. A reinsurance of reinsurance by one reinsurer (the retrocedent) to another (the retrocessionaire).

Room, The. The underwriting room at Lloyd's.

Rota Committee. The Lloyd's committee that considers applications for underwriting membership or for admission as a Lloyd's broker or underwriting agent.

Salvage. Saving property from loss or destruction; or property saved.

Salvage charges. Compensation payable for saving, or attempting to save, property at sea from loss or destruction.

SG form of policy. The traditional form of Lloyd's marine insurance policy, known by the initials at its head which stand for ship and goods.

Ship classification. The grading of ships by their attributes.

Signing slip. The brokers' slip used for submitting details to the Lloyd's Policy Signing Office, so that an insurance may be recorded for signing or accounting purposes. It may be the original slip, a certified photocopy or an initialled off slip.

Slip. A document submitted by a broker to an underwriter containing details of a proposed insurance set out in concise form.

Slip policy. A broker's slip signed by the Lloyd's Policy Signing Office for use as evidence of an insurance in lieu of a policy.

Special reserve fund. A reserve in which a proportion of underwriting profit may be put, thus deferring liability for higher rate income tax.

Special settlement. The procedure whereby a particular premium or claim is paid outside the usual monthly settlement, usually within seven days.

Stop-loss reinsurance. A form of reinsurance whereby the reinsurer pays losses in any year to the extent that they exceed some stated proportion of premiums.

Subrogation. The right of an underwriter to exercise any rights of the insured against a third party in mitigation of a claim the underwriter has met.

Subscriber. Originally all members of Lloyd's were termed subscribers. Nowadays the term is limited to individuals employed by a Lloyd's broker or underwriting agency who are elected as annual subscribers with entry to the Room, but with no power to underwrite.

Substitute. A person admitted to the underwriting Room at Lloyd's as an employee of an underwriter or broker.

Surplus line. Business surplus to the capacity of a local insurance market, especially in the United States.

Surplus reinsurance. Reinsurance to cover that part of an insurance that is in excess of the proportion the original insurer wishes to retain.

Syndicate. A group of underwriters on whose behalf insurances are accepted, each underwriter taking a proportion for himself without assuming liability for the proportions of other syndicate members.

Tariff company. An insurance company that has agreed with other companies to charge rates of premium not less than those indicated in a table (or tariff) of rates.

t.b.a. To be advised or to be agreed. Letters used on a slip where further information or negotiations are necessary.

Third party. A person who is not a party to a contract.

Three-year accounting. A system of insurance accounting under which profits or losses for a given year are not determined until the end of three years.

Time policy. A marine insurance policy running for a specified period.

Tonner policy. A policy, now forbidden at Lloyd's, for payment of a fixed sum upon the loss of a ship of specified tonnage or an aircraft of specified value or type, regardless of whether the insured has an insurable interest or has lost.

Treaty reinsurance. Reinsurance under a contract (treaty) relating to the whole or a section of the insured's business over a period.

Tribunalisation. A financial vetting by an underwriters' association of someone to whom a Lloyd's syndicate contemplates issuing a binding authority.

Uberrima fides. The utmost good faith (Lloyd's motto).

Underwriter. An underwriting member of Lloyd's; or one whose business it is to consider proposals for insurance on behalf of a syndicate or insurance company.

Underwriting agent. A person, partnership or company that carries out the duties of a *Managing agent* or a *Members' agent* or of both.

Voyage policy. A marine insurance policy in respect of a specified voyage.

Waiter. A porter or messenger at Lloyd's.

Warranty. An undertaking by the insured that some particular thing shall or shall not be done, or that some condition shall be fulfilled or that particular facts are affirmed or negatived. A breach entitles the insurer to deny liability; or a limitation of cover imposed by an insurer.

Weather insurance. Insurance against loss by adverse weather conditions, for example, rainfall causing the abandonment of an outside sporting event.

Without prejudice. A term used in discussions intended to guard against any inference of waiver of right on the part of the party using it.

Working member. An underwriting member who occupies himself principally with the conduct of business at Lloyd's by a Lloyd's broker or underwriting agent, or who, having retired, did so immediately before retirement.

INDEX

153

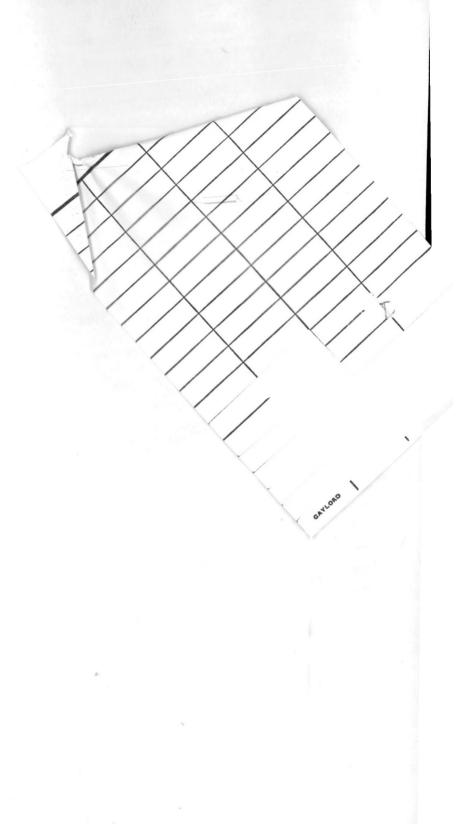

GAYLORD